"I chose to come here;
I chose to tell a story;
I brought love and stories here."

SADAGAT ALIYEVA

WE THE INTER WOVEN

AN ANTHOLOGY OF BICULTURAL IOWA

SADAGAT ALIYEVA
MELISSA PALMA
CHUY RENTERIA

EDITOR ANDREA WILSON

Published by the Iowa Writers' House
www.iowawritershouse.org

The BIWF program and *We the Interwoven* was made possible
by an Art Project Grant from the Iowa Arts Council
and the National Endowment for the Arts.

First Edition

Author photos by Miriam Alarcón Avila and Sarah Smith

Set in Garamond, Futura, and Painting with Chocolate

Designed by Skylar Alexander Moore

Printed by Total Printing Systems

ISBN 978-1-732406-0-1

CONTENTS

FOREWORD

Iowa has long been home to people of many lands, from indigenous peoples, including our namesake, the Ioway; to European settlers making their way west; to new populations arriving today from Latin America, Southeast Asia, West Africa, and beyond. Whether they came for the promise of agricultural work or picturesque family life, for a fresh start or for a return to generational roots, all have become part of the fabric of our state, interweaving to form a vivid tapestry of diverse cultures that make up the greater culture of Iowa. While often overlooked as a flyover state, our fields of opportunity quietly house the dreams of residents from all backgrounds as we continue to evolve what it means to be of this place.

The Bicultural Iowa Writers' Fellowship (BIWF) was created to bring to light the writing of Iowans who are both of this place and of another. It is the only program of its kind in the state—a fully funded residency that provides the training and the platform for telling these essential stories.

The program's inaugural fellows are individuals as artists and as people, but they all have one thing in common: they call Iowa home. Each artist uses the genres that their talents most naturally express. Chuy Renteria found his voice best expressed in essay and short fiction, while Melissa Palma chose a combination of poetry, fiction, and essays to tell her stories. Sadagat Aliyeva gifts us not only with her mystical fables but also with a talent in illustration unlike any we've yet seen.

This collection represents their unique experiences and amalgamation of influences, from the coast of Azerbaijan to the border towns of Mexico to the archipelago of the Philippines, all now firmly rooted here in the heartland.

In these times it may be easy to fall back into divisions of Self and Other, but the stories in this book remind us that the experiences of being human are grounded in universal truths that we all share. Life, liberty, and the pursuit of happiness are the founding ideals of this nation, and we hope this collection encourages all of us to ensure these unalienable rights are extended to everyone.

ANDREA WILSON
Founder, Iowa Writers' House

ACKNOWLEDGMENTS

The Bicultural Iowa Writers' Fellowship (BIWF) and resulting collection owes itself to a great many people:

To Hugh Ferrer of the International Writing Program and to Iowa Poet Laureate Mary Swander for their early support and believing in the vision.

To Lucas Benson and Katie Roche for their passionate support as we sought grant funding for the BIWF program.

To Maggie Conroy, Jennifer Fawcett, and Alisha Jeddeloh for giving their time and talent to the fellowship experience.

To Iowa State University students Amalie Kwassman, Kartika Budhwar, and Danielle Buchanan for their contributions as student readers and to professor Jennifer Knox for the student connections.

To Ana Merino of the University of Iowa Spanish Creative Writing Program and Aron Aji of the Translation Program for connecting us with translation assistance, and to Nieves Lopez Martin, Marissa Bender, and Sergio Maldonado for their translations and in-language proofreading.

To Alisha Jeddeloh for copyediting.

To Skylar Alexander for the beauty of our book.

To the Iowa Arts Council and the National Endowment for the Arts for making this entire program possible.

To the supporters of the Iowa Writers' House for believing in our organization and helping us get these stories out into the world.

To the Iowa literary community and the City of Literature for celebrating the Writers' House as an essential part of our literary world.

CHUY RENTERIA

ARTIST STATEMENT

I grew up believing that my life was a conduit to making art. My small hometown of West Liberty, Iowa, nurtured that belief. Where cultures of people coexisted as litmus tests for America at large. Where Mexican and Laotian immigrants intermingled with small-town Midwestern values.

I learned to draw before I could walk. Started my twenty-year dance career before learning how to drive. Began writing before I realized how important my perspective was to the collective.

I have always wanted to use these forms to describe how it feels to be who I am. To document the passion of the people around me. To champion vibrant, messy cultural experience not reflected in popular culture.

Ultimately I want my output to represent visceral humanness. Prose describing awkward cross-cultural exchanges. Ephemeral dances into the twilight of my career. I hope that people who experience my stories feel pangs of remembrance. That they see the root of our collective story.

A STORY ABOUT WORK

Chuy Renteria

LET ME TELL YOU about my relationship with work. 'Cause if you're Mexican in America, you have a relationship with work. And it doesn't matter if you're first generation, third, undocumented, or anything in between, it's a complicated relationship. If you're Mexican in America, work isn't just work. Work is how people look at you if you have an accent. Work is how dark you get when you work construction. Work is what happens when you are a bunch of Mexicans on the roof of a white person's house. *Paisas* and coconuts—undocumented middle-aged men and college kids who can't speak Spanish—all on one roof. But to the people driving along the road, we're one and the same and hidden. Mexicans on a roof, doing a job the drivers would rather not do.

One of the first jobs I had was at the grocery store. Produce section. I applied and they responded the same day. The conversation started with technicalities, availability and contacts, but veered when the HR person on the phone asked if I was responding to their ad. I wasn't. I just needed a job and applied. The ad was for individuals who could speak English and Spanish. I don't remember if they asked for Mexican-Americans specifically, I don't know if they can legally do that, but that was exactly what they were looking for. HR lady asked me point blank: "You can speak to our Spanish-speaking customers then, right?"

If we have a strained relationship with work, then first-generation Mexican-Americans feel that strain compounded due to Spanish. Here's the thing: I can understand Spanish . . . for the most part . . . the percentage number I throw out is 80 percent understanding. My parents talk to me all in Spanish and I reply with this jilted, jagged Spanglish. It's for the most part English with a few *peros* and *comos* peppered throughout. My wife even pointed out that my English changes when I talk to my parents, it becomes simpler, I have an accent. I didn't realize this until she told me. A sample reply to my parents' questions could be, "No, I worked long . . . *pero*, I didn't know when. *Cuando . . . eight . . . como a la ocho.* Yeah . . . yeah.

3

No se, I don't know."

My code switching is misfires. Buttons that stick and repeat themselves. But I can understand about 80 to 85 percent of what my parents actually say. It amazes white people when I point it out. "Yeah, my older brother speaks fluently. His oldest kid doesn't want to speak Spanish but his youngest son does. My sister's kids don't speak at all, even though she's the most Mexican out of us all." That's a thing we ask ourselves: How Mexican are you really?

That sentiment was racing through my mind when HR lady asked me her simple question, of whether I could speak Spanish. I stammered. "Well . . . yeah, yeah I can understand it. I don't know how well I could speak on fruits and vegetables though." I learned through Duolingo that the Spanish word for carrot is *zanahoria.* My *tía* used it in a sentence a week later and the serendipity blew my mind. I tried to break down the 80 percent understanding/not-so-good-at-speaking rubric to the HR lady. She spoke some HR talk that amounted to, "Good enough."

After I got the job, my manager asked me if I wanted to pose for some photos for some advertisements, the weekly coupons the grocery store sends out on Sundays. "Sure, why not," I told myself and posed by the oranges, cheesing for the camera. A couple of weeks later my friend Pepe told me the news.

"Hey, I saw you in the paper the other day for your work," he said.

"Oh yeah, I forgot that they took those pictures, how did they turn out?" I asked.

"They're alright. You look hilarious. Posing. Saying some things that you would never say."

"What? About the produce?"

"Yeah, that too, but I mean, the fact that they got you speaking Spanish like you know it!"

I full-out sprinted to my house. Tore through the newspaper on the kitchen table. There I was. Orange in my hand. Thick blocks of Spanish text emanating from a speech bubble above my head. Words I had trouble reading, let alone speaking fluently. It was something like how quality the produce was. How if you ever needed help,

4

come find someone who looks like me, wink wink. "Oh shit," I thought to myself. My girlfriend's mom, who was white, thought I looked great in the ad and put it up on the fridge. My mom did not.

I did actually have a few encounters with Spanish speakers in the grocery aisles, with varying levels of success. Once again, I can understand things pretty well, and the level of discourse on topics like trying to find the price of jalapeños is pretty basic. There was one Mexican lady that I fucked up with. She was asking about a discount on some canned food and my Spanglish came out hard. I couldn't for the life of me remember the word for fifty. *Cincuenta.* Instead of saying "No, no. This is fifty cents off," I was saying something close to "This is five and zero off. Five and zero . . . *cinco y zero.*" She got frustrated and left me in the aisle, not before asking where I was from and *who my mother was.* (How Mexican are you? How Mexican is your mom for having raised you?) I didn't stay much longer at the grocery store.

After that I had a string of summer jobs. I was taking classes at Kirkwood and every summer came to the same conclusion that I was broke as a joke. Looking back now, the jobs I chose were interesting. I must've had this string of wanting to take on jobs that were stereotypically Mexican. I worked as a custodian, in a back dock for a clothes store, as a dishwasher. Deep down, I had a chip on my shoulder. Like I was the Mexican Matt Damon in *Good Will Hunting,* mop in my hand. I got a weird kick out of white people coming up to me as I cleaned. I assumed that they assumed I didn't speak English. I was unnecessarily verbose when giving replies, like a kid who recently discovered a thesaurus. I'm not even sure if people noticed my answers, or even me in general. Give a Mexican a mop in a store and watch them disappear before your eyes. Plus, when someone is asking for the bathroom, they usually tear off as soon as they see you point the way.

I have to be careful here about how I recall these jobs. These were tough jobs and I learned a lot from them. I argue to this day that there is honor in cleaning and doing the work that others will not do. There is catharsis and pride in manual labor that no desk job can match. There's a section in *Anna Karenina* where it goes into hyper detail about a character working the field. I've heard people talk about how boring this section is. I was almost brought to tears. Like I said, we have a complicated relationship with work.

There is one good story from my time in the back dock of the clothing department store. That job was a family affair. My mom got the job first and pitched it to me and my brother, Johnny. Soon we got my cousin Gable to join in on the gig. The clothes would arrive in semitrucks in the back docks. We would unload them from the trucks, put them on Z racks, long yellow racks on wheels, then take them out to the various departments to slang. The wheels of the rack would screech as we wheeled them under the fluorescent lights. It was all pretty simple and carefree. For the most part people left us alone. Our manager was kind of a tool, an outcast from the rest of the department for sure, but the boss of us. He would later refer to this story I'm about to tell as *the incident*.

The incident goes like this. It was close to the end of the day and I was the last one left in the back dock. I was cleaning up some odds and ends, stuffing cardboard into a chute, when a sales associate came bursting through the doors.

"So what's going on over here? I've been trying to call *you guys* for the last fifteen minutes and the phone has been busy this whole time?" she said. I looked over at the bright yellow phone on the dock wall. This is the phone that the sales associates would call us on when they wanted us to bring over some Z racks. I'm looking at the phone and I can see that it's very slightly off its hook. I'm thinking about who was the last person to hang up the phone . . . was it Gable, maybe my mo—

"Hello!?" the associate cut off my train of thinking. "So *you guys* are back here and trying to get out of helping us out? What am I saying, do you even understand English?"

That was it. That was the question. I want to say that I said the following. I honestly do not remember, but I wish, I wish that I had said this: "Yes. I can understand English, I can probably speak it better than you." My memory fails me. Rethinking on this memory, fantasizing on what I could have said clouds things. Clouds whether I actually said it or not. It's one of the handful of shower memories I have. The memories that hit you all at once in the shower. To remember and reenact scenarios in the steam. "Even if I don't

6

understand English, I know enough not to be so fucking rude!" is another response I reenact. I know I did not say that one.

What I did say was, "Yeah, I do . . . sorry, I didn't realize the phone—" as she snatched the Z rack and took it from the dock. I remember feeling helpless. As helpless as when I first went to elementary school and was too shy to speak. You know that game, two truths and a lie? My friend Ruben calls it a "parlor game." You tell two truths and a lie to try to stumble people up. One of my go-to truths to trip people up is this: "When I first went to elementary school, I didn't know any English and would only speak with my parents in Spanish." I told this to my advanced university Spanish class. This was the class that I tried to CLEP out of but had to take for my language credit. I told them this factoid and they couldn't believe it. They had experienced my Spanglish, my red-cheeked conjugation. There was no way this one was the lie. I still don't know whether it's true or not; my parents insist that it was. I think it had more to do with being shy, but either way I remember landing in the ESL class and crying.

Which brings me back to *the incident.* The incident wasn't this exchange. The incident was the Steinbeckian letter that I wrote afterward. I took that helplessness, as she tore away the Z rack, and found the closest pad and pen. It was my *Good Will Hunting* moment, my Mexican "How 'bout dem apples?" I wrote out our exchange, including the "Do you even understand English?", and talked about how we, the dock workers, put up with so much. I talked about going back to community college, I talked about equality. I let it fly. Signed it with my full name, walked over to the head manager of the entire store, and slipped it under her door. A week later HR reprimanded the associate and told her to take a couple days off to cope. My mom still talks about the incident. She and the rest of my family couldn't stop talking about it.

"Good!" my mom would say. "They needed to hear that so they know that we're actually people." I wrote another letter a couple weeks later, this one to the dock manager. To let him know I was quitting for good.

These side jobs and incidents are insights into my relationship with work. Work means something different to us here. It's

7

complicated. It reveals things about how you look at yourself, about how you feel others look at you. There's one job I had that encapsulates this feeling: roofing with my brother.

It was the summer after the department store gig. After another year of community college. I hated going to that college. I was an average high school student and did not have the grades to get into the university proper. My good friends went to the University of Iowa, one on a wrestling scholarship, the other through sheer scholastic achievement. I looked at community college as an albatross from not taking things as seriously as I could have in high school. Which is not to say I tried any harder at Kirkwood. It took me four and a half years to get my two-year associate's degree. One time I caught my mom humblebragging to a neighbor that I had been going to college for X amount of years. To her, the more time you spent studying at college, the better. Doctors spend decades going to school, right? The neighbor and I didn't have the heart to tell my mom that a physician's course load wasn't the same as me flunking out of algebra a second time.

So it was always good to finish up in the spring and get back to the hobbies and openness of summer. Close to the end of the semester, Charlie, one of Kirkwood's advisement staff, found me in the commons area. Charlie was one of the nicest people I've ever met. Tall guy with glasses, who looked to always be on the precipice of a genuine smile. All you had to do was give him a reason. Tell him about your day, or what career you wanted to work in, and he would pat your shoulder and break out into that smile. Charlie, in suit jackets with shoulder pads, would spend his lunch breaks in the commons area. He'd catch up with every student he could in that hour. He always remembered my name, even recently, after not seeing me for the better part of a decade. Turns out he used to call my high school track meets. He said, "How could I forget a name like *Hey-zeus?*"

Anyway, Charlie checked in with me at the commons. Asked how I was doing and if I had any plans for the summer. I told him that I'd be chilling, but I usually tried to find a summer job for some extra cash. "Of course, gotta make some extra dough, right? Well, let me know how it goes? What adventures you get yourself into!"

8

Charlie said with a laugh as he slapped my shoulder.

Charlie's inquiry into my summer plans was on my mind while I found a job listing online. All signs pointed to it being a sales associate position. I walked into the offices and realized too late that it was one of those weird pyramid schemes where they try to get you to sell knives to your friends and family. The first "training" meeting was them trying to convince us why we needed to buy the knife set ourselves to understand the product. We'd have to pay for the knives and training to use them. Of course.

I told my mom about this, and she laughed and told me what a crock it was. Their receptionist called every weekday for three weeks after the first "interview." *They* were calling *me,* so you know it was a scheme. After finishing laughing, my mom got out that I should work roofing with my brother, Johnny. He was back in town from Texas and had a gig lined up. I should talk to him. The next morning Johnny woke me up at six in the morning for my first day roofing.

I still had sleep in my eyes as he drove his huge Ford F-150 down the highway. The house we were going to was about forty-five minutes from our hometown of West Liberty. My brother is ten years older than me, so at the time he was hitting thirty, about the same age I am now.

Man, I used to worship Johnny as a kid. He would drive me to school in his black Firebird. Blast Rage Against the Machine as he pulled up to my middle school. I thought it was the coolest shit in the world. Zach de la Rocha is another Mexican like us, caught in the middle. I never got the full story, but either Johnny or one of his friends crashed that Firebird, wasted.

Johnny got caught with too many drugs in his apartment a couple years before our summer roofing together. He drove off to Odessa, Texas, to work in the oil fields with my *tíos* and keep a low profile. The high school football show *Friday Night Lights* takes place in a fictionalized Odessa, though my *tíos* told us that all the Mexicans go to the poorer high school with a shitty football team.

Anyway, Johnny came back for Christmas that year. The police pulled him over for having an out-of-state license plate. Then they saw he had a warrant for an arrest and threw him in the city jail for a couple months. I remember him walking through our door the evening he got out, glassy eyed, with a scraggly beard he'd never had before or since. He was out now and stuck in Iowa, court case pending, looking for work. Him and I would find it together. That's not to say that he talked to me about any of this. Our family coexists between the cracks of discourse. Pregnant pauses as we think of things less personal to say.

Usually the less personal discussion is about the work ahead. As we drove along the highway, the conversation turned to that. Johnny said, "Alright, so here's the deal. I met this guy, right? Big old white guy. He manages a couple of teams, does roofing, siding, all that shit, right? His name is Joe. This guy used to be the real deal. Now he's lost in the sauce. Too much drink. You'll see him, watch. He walks around like a chicken with his head cut off." I remember this phrase. I remember how it was the perfect encapsulation of Joe's being.

"So here's our plan," Johnny continued. "While this guy is dicking around with his various crews, we go in and do work. This guy Joe doesn't get how fast we can get this shit done. There's money here and we can work it right and get it."

My brother was laying out his game plan as if it was this nefarious scheme. I didn't get why doing the work better than Joe anticipated could be this underhanded thing. But I had never seen my brother work. When you work faster, harder, and smarter than anyone expects, there are ways to push past your superiors. When this work is something as unregulated as roofing and construction jobs, then you find ways to get paid that your drunken superior doesn't see. "Get in with the homeowners, let Joe's old connections open the door for us, leave drunken Joe outside."

Roofing, like most real tough jobs, is pretty simple. You can learn the gist of the entire process in a day. You can grab a person off the street and have them tear down old shingles with a thirty-second demonstration, which is what Johnny taught me that first morning. Tear down is like this: you grab a pitchfork or a roofing shovel/shingle remover, you get on the roof, and you rip off the shingles from the bottom up. You got to push and scrape under the shingles. To get underneath the nails. Then you leverage your shovel and pry the shingles off. When you get good at it, you can pry big chunks of shingles from the roof. You start at the bottom of the roof and work your way up. It's grunt work. Necessary and taxing. After tearing off, you heave the chunks of debris onto a tarp or dumpster below. Finesse comes into play when you deal with the felt underneath the shingles. The layers of a roof, from the most superficial to the deepest, goes shingles, felt, then plywood. The felt is there to waterproof the house. If you rip into the old felt before you roll new felt on, this could be a problem. Especially if you don't have any new rolls of felt at hand and there's a chance of rain that day. There's many a scolded grunt for being too careless when tearing down and ripping the felt up to shit.

After tear down, you have to get the new shingles onto the roof. Other people use mechanical lifts to plop dozens of shingle bundles on a roof. We had to hoist the eighty-pound bundles over our shoulders and climb the ladder ourselves. We made games of it—see who could ascend the ladder the smoothest or who could carry the most bundles in a day.

My brother taught me the basics on the roofs of cookie-cutter condos in North Liberty. After a couple weeks we started to amass a squad of misfits to lay out Johnny's plan. I talked my cousins Tony and Mark into joining us. Tony and Mark were both a year younger than me and dancers in my breaking crew. We three were inseparable that summer, so it made sense to get them to join us and make some money. Tony and Mark were cousins of mine like almost everyone in West Liberty is your cousin. In other words, we weren't actually cousins. Hear me out. Somewhere in the family trees, one of my mom's *tías* is the half sister to one of their dad's cousins. But by the white definition of the word, we were best friends who said we were cousins. It was easier to say so than to trace the mangled roots of our family trees. Tony and Mark were out of high school, always arguing or goofing off, and as clueless as I was to the real world. We were the bottom-of-the-barrel grunts and too young to realize how much that actually sucked.

One morning, on the caravan to pick everyone up, Johnny said that he was grabbing Malcolm, one of his old friends. When our F-150 pulled up to the condo in Iowa City to pick Malcolm up, Mark was the first to notice the familiar face.

"Oh hey, that's James Truth!" Mark said as he got out to meet Malcolm/James.

"Is that what he's going by nowadays?" Johnny asked as Tony followed Mark to give James some dap. James Truth was the rapper stage name of Malcolm, Johnny's old friend from his Iowa City days before the arrest. We knew James Truth from the hip-hop circuit. We were all part of a monthly hip-hop showcase. James would rap and our crew would break during intermissions. James was dark, handsome, smooth talking, and a pretty good performer. He fashioned himself after the the rapper/singers of the time. 50 Cent. The Game.

"Doesn't matter what he goes by as long as he can still hold it down with a nail gun," Johnny said before the trio piled into the truck.

Turned out Malcolm could still work a nail gun and lay shingles down. Not as good as Johnny, but good enough to be an asset to the team. What separates the grunts from the skilled roofers is what happens after you're done tearing off and placing felt down. It's when you actually have to lay down new shingles. The skilled guys can place shingles down and secure them in place fast with a nail gun. You could tell how good a person was with a nail gun by the rhythm and pacing of the nails firing each shingle in place. Malcolm was good: his nail gun would be at a steady pop . . . pop . . . pop before he took a beat to slap on the next shingle and repeat the process. Johnny was a master. He would line up all his shingles in a row and smoothly shift to each one on his knees.

Poppoppop-poppoppop-poppoppop—All along the roof. Johnny and Malcolm carried old foam couch cushions to rest their knees on while nail gunning. If you were fancy you would get some knee pads, but we made do with what we had.

Johnny and Malcolm would reminisce about old days between nail-gun shots. Tony, Mark, and I would wipe away sweat and dirt from our faces and talk about what new trouble we could get into during the weekends. We would all have calluses and bruises from lifting bundles up ladders. Cuts and scrapes from bumping into nail and debris. The smell of tar and dust filled our nostrils as we worked

12

in stifling heat. We would crack jokes at each other's expense and get paid on a semi-regular basis. It was getting close to Johnny's original plan. Drunken Joe would give us a new roofing job to do, we would get it finished close to or better than the estimated time. And repeat.

We would get paid in cash, of course. There were no W2s, no insurance, and no taxes for the type of roofing we were doing. Paychecks were rolls of cash transferred from Joe's bank account to Johnny's hand. Johnny would then divvy up the sum to his team. I remember getting paid for the first time. I mean paid. It wasn't like the paychecks at the grocery store; checks for seven dollars an hour for fifteen-hour work weeks. The first time I got paid roofing, Johnny handed me the most money I had ever held in my hand. Tony, Mark, and I spent it like kids working summer jobs living at home do, on games, clothes, movies, and other things we didn't need but felt good spending money on.

My brother was saving his money up. I didn't think much about it at the time but had to have known the reason for Johnny's plan in the first place. My cousins and I enjoyed the extra spending money to burn, but my brother *needed* this money. For bills. For lawyer fees. To get the fuck out of Iowa and on with his life. I think back on the rhythm of his nail gun and hear his desperation in trying to get ahead of his past. *Poppoppop-poppoppop.*

And we were getting ahead at first, getting ahead of schedule, finishing jobs faster than Joe could find them. We were getting paid. Joe even gave us bigger cuts 'cause he was happy with us.

"You guys are fast, not like the other teams I got," Joe would say to us each time he got our money out of the bank. Joe would usually have me drive him for these bank runs since he started cracking open Busch Lights around eight in the morning. I didn't mind being his chauffeur, because that meant getting away from manual labor and closer to cash in my pocket.

Those first couple of weeks were simple and as fun as you could get doing manual labor. We worked fast and got paid. Joe mainly stayed out of our way besides sometimes wobbling up a ladder to inspect our work. We all got darker. We started to notice that girls started to notice that we were getting fitter. I hated eating heavy during lunch breaks 'cause that would make the last stretch of the day a slog. So I stuck to salad, chicken, and water. My diet and work load put me in one of the best shapes of my life.

One particularly sunny day, Johnny busted out some sunblock. He handed it to Malcolm.

"Come on now. I've never known any black man to use that stuff once in his life," Malcolm said as he tossed it over to me. I looked at the way the tattoos on his arm hid in the tone of his skin, then over to the blue bottle in my hand.

"I've never used this stuff before either," I said as I tossed it back to Johnny.

"You sure, man? You're not trying to look cool in front of Malcolm, are you?" Johnny replied. It was true though. I remember being in awe at how much sunblock my white friends had to put on at the Kimberly Park pool. They in turn would marvel at how dark I got while the spots they missed turned pink and cracked. Tony, Mark, and I took off our shirts and worked in the sun all day for maximum tanning results.

The next day my back felt itchy as I sat in the back seat of the truck. We would start working early enough in the day that it was still cold out. By nine or ten in the morning it was warm enough to take off our hoodies. By half past eleven it was hot and we took off our shirts again.

"Holy. Shit. Man, your back's all burnt up!" Mark said to me while getting Tony's attention. Noticing Mark's back, I immediately realized how mine must have looked.

"Aw man, do I look as dumb as you two?" Tony asked before I could. We had managed to completely sunburn our entire backs. But since we were working on the roof with our backs toward the sun the whole day, the fronts of our bodies were pale. We looked like three miserable lobsters, red backs and white bellies. Johnny and Malcolm cracked up from their spots on the roof.

We kept our pace through June and into July. We did roofs in Iowa City, North Liberty, Cedar Rapids, and tons of little towns in southeast Iowa. I dealt with my fear of heights on this three-story monstrosity of a roof. We had to nail pieces of two-by-fours onto the roof to walk along 'cause the angle was so steep.

Everything was going good until Joe started noticing the money that we were making. That's how it works. I mean Joe noticing in the way someone notices that they can make *more* money off someone. Things started to get crunchy when Joe started to hoist new members into our crew. The first new person Joe introduced was this guy named Darren. The entire summer that I roofed, Darren was the only white guy who was there as our equal, meaning he didn't consider himself to be over us in any way and was actually proud to work with us. He was middle aged and sinewy with a stutter. He was a grunt but worked hard. Darren liked to show how hip he was by using Mexican slang and talking about all the different types of woman he was into. "It don't matter *guey* I'll t-talk to any *mami,*" Darren would say during breaks, our legs dangling off the side of the roof.

On a cloudy day in Mt. Vernon, Joe came up to us to talk about the last member he wanted to join our team. Cloudy days were tricky 'cause Johnny would be on edge that it might start raining. Then we would have to tarp over any unshingled areas of the roof and call it a day. A day off was fine for most of us, but to Johnny it meant another day slowed down from finishing a project. Joe walked over to Johnny, smelling of cheap beer.

"Alright, so there's this guy that I got coming onto our team, Johnny," Joe said as he walked up. Johnny hid a smirk as he reacted to the "our team" part of that statement.

"Oh yeah? We gonna get someone that can actually handle a nail gun this time?" Johnny replied.

"Of course, of course. Let me tell you, Johnny. This guy is an illegal, right? And you know me, I don't give two shits whether you're illegal or legal or from fuckin' Mars as long as you can work." Johnny put down his nail gun and sat on his foam pad to look over at Joe. "And this guy Arturo, he used to work for me, and I tell ya, he was the best damn worker I've ever had. Could finish a whole roof off on his own if you gave him a day."

Johnny laughed. "Alright then. I'm not gonna argue with that. When's he start?"

"Well, here's the thing, Arturo got tied up in some shit back in

15

Mexico. I don't know what it is with you people, but he got himself into a mess and can't get here. Damn shame too, 'cause I told him there's money to be made. So Arturo is sending his brother to work in his place."

"And he's good?" Johnny asked.

"If he's half the worker Arturo was, then he'll be good enough for our team." Joe said as he ran his hand through his messy graying hair and blew a snot rocket off the roof.

A week later Arturo's brother, Ignacio, showed up at our house at seven in the morning ready to work.

"Alright, let's see what this Mexican can do," Johnny said to me as he filled his thermos with coffee before we piled into his truck. At this point Johnny relegated Tony and Mark to the bed of the truck, among the piles of shingles and tools. They cracked jokes to each other in the passing wind.

Turned out Ignacio wasn't quite half the worker Arturo was. He fell somewhere between Malcolm and Johnny in competency with a nail gun. He wasn't the master gunslinger that my brother hoped for. Ignacio was the adequate sheriff's deputy to Johnny's Cisco Kid. But he equaled out our ratio of gunners to grunts. There was Malcolm, Johnny, and Ignacio nailing the sections of roofs that Tony, Mark, Darren, and I would tear off.

Johnny translated for Ignacio to the rest of us. Johnny was fluent in Spanish and let Ignacio in on our plans for the summer. At this point we were pulling way ahead of scheduled projects. One day I watched as Johnny made his move below with the owner of a house. Johnny talked to him about the project we finished and said, "Hey, if you know of anyone else that needs work done, give them my number." At this point the homeowner knew that Johnny was the one actually calling the shots.

"Yeah, you know Joe used to be a respectable guy," the owner confided to Johnny. "Now he's gotten too deep into the drink. Deep down that guy is still in there . . . but what was your number again?" Johnny gave it to him and they shook hands.

Pretty soon we were adding side projects that Joe wasn't privy to. Johnny would split us up, three of us working here, four of us working there for a day. We were making bank. Even though Ignacio was not his fabled brother Arturo, he was enough for us to ramp up our speed. Our group started to hit our groove.

Until we hit this house in West Liberty. It was a new house under construction, which should have made it easier. Johnny actually went to high school with the owner of the house.

"Oh wow. Never thought you'd be one of the guys working on my new house!" the guy jovially said to Johnny the first day our ragtag group walked on his property.

There was something about this house that brought the worst luck. Tony and Mark started throwing around the word *cursed. The House on the Hill.* It rained on and off the first week we started. A pallet of shingles Joe got for us were all rotted and unusable. There was a high amount of accidents on the site. We started to fall behind on schedule.

The House on the Hill was shaping up to be American wholesomeness on the outside. It was the inside of the house that was causing our bad luck. The cutting of corners on the construction caused our misfortune. Johnny pointed out some of the shoddy workmanship that went into the house.

"I'm shaking my damn head at some of the things I'm seeing. Look at this. Dude is trying to cut all these corners and be cheap but still look nice. Why not get the work done right the first time?" Johnny said.

To be honest, I didn't really notice some of the things my brother was pointing out. Over the summer I came to learn one of the fundamental differences between us. When it came to roofing, Johnny had an intense pride in his work and the finished output. He would comment on botched roof jobs we passed by. Or divulge how he would've gotten construction jobs done in simpler and more cost-effective ways. Or make us redo the chalk lines we snapped onto the felt of a roof. Over and over again. Until it was right. At times it felt like being on the set of a Stanley Kubrick movie with the same notorious attention to detail. I'm imagining the reshoots on the set of *2001* as Stanley makes the apes carry shingles up the ladder *just right.*

The only time Johnny handed the three cousins a nail gun, one of us had misaligned a shingle and added an extra nail. This was on a random part of a roof that no owner would have seen. Johnny made us tear down the entire row of shingles and lay down a perfect new row.

"We have to prove that we can do this shit right. Have pride in your work," he would say to us. To himself.

The day I shocked my arm on an exposed wire, we had to cut the work early. Not because of the accident, but because we were getting well into July and it was getting hot. Waves-of-heat-dancing-in-the-sky hot. So hot that as we walked on the roof, our boots left tar footprints on the shingles. At first Johnny told us to walk with our whole feet on the roof and be careful. But after Darren and I left a particularly noticeable trail, Johnny had us quit.

"This is fucked. We're going to have to redo this entire roof," Johnny said. I tried to hide my eye roll as I made my way down the ladder.

A difference in new-construction homes is there are lots of little teams working beside each other. There was the group of guys doing the siding of the house, the legitimate crew pouring the concrete for the driveway, electricians, and so on. As my brother and I traded passive-aggressive barbs over the tracks on the roof, we passed by one of these other crews. They were a group of white high school kids plastering the inside of the home's garage. The kids ignored my brother and I, and our cousins walking beside us. Getting ignored by the other groups on a site—hell, from everyone—was common. It was like my janitorial days—you sort of vanish when you're working.

But it was different when the high school kids saw Malcolm. I looked on as one of the kids nudged another to get his attention. They attempted to brush off some of the plaster caked on their clothes as they made there way over to James Truth.

"Ay yo, man you got a cigarette?" one of them asked. I suspected they already knew that he indeed did. The two kids ended up talking to Malcolm for the better part of fifteen minutes. It ended with one of the kids showcasing some of his raps as Malcolm looked on and laughed.

As we walked to the truck, finished for the day as the temperature was still rising, Johnny asked Malcolm, "What was that all about?"

"Gotta give them what they want. They said they'd be at my next show," James replied.

After a couple more mishaps, we finished that cursed house way behind schedule. We were happy to finish and move on, especially since not having done any other jobs meant we were that much further from getting paid. We started a new house in Iowa City and picked up the pace. Joe usually paid us on Fridays, even if we got jobs done earlier. It was his way of trying to keep things official feeling. The Friday on the new Iowa City job came and went. Then another Friday. We were well into July without a cent to show for the cursed house. Joe kept giving Johnny excuses. Talking about how this other crew he had was asking for money too and how Joe had some plans lined up to get all us paid.

Tony and Mark started talking to Ignacio, teaching him English words like they taught Darren Spanish. Ignacio asked them how to say "Pay me" in English.

Mark replied, "Nah, nah, for now with Joe it should go: Fuck you. Pay me."

Ignacio repeated the line with a heavy accent, his hands outstretched on the roof. *"Ay pinche Joe. Fuck you. Pay me!"*

Tony, Mark, and Ignacio all laughed as they took turns demanding money from an invisible Joe on the roof. Johnny's nail gun cut through the air in even rhythms.

As we finished our last job in July with no payout in sight, things started to get tense. Tony and Mark even caught dour moods as they stopped goofing around on the job. We had a couple days where we all worked in relative silence, the ambient noise of cars passing and birds chirping mixed with the clanking of our tools.

Finally one Saturday Ignacio had enough. He came knocking at our house in the afternoon. As I opened the front door he immediately starting speaking rapid-fire Spanish. I couldn't catch everything but could tell he was angry. I tried to slow him down as he continued to rant until finally Ignacio slowed down and pointed past me, indicating that he was talking about my brother.

"Fuck *you*. Pay me," he said before walking off in disgust.

19

I mentioned this to Johnny later that night. "I keep on telling him that Joe keeps on ducking me," Johnny said. "We're all hurting here, not just him." I looked over at the video games I had bought the month earlier and changed the subject.

It wasn't too long after this incident that Ignacio left the group permanently. Turned out he was sending most of his cash to help get his brother out of trouble in Mexico. With the little cash left over, he rented an apartment behind a laundromat downtown. It was a utility closet that someone converted into a "studio apartment." Ignacio sent too much money back home and couldn't cover the rent for August. They kicked him out and kept the deposit. If Kurt Vonnegut were Mexican, would he still say "So it goes," or maybe *"Así pasa"*?

If our output stalled after the cursed house, it crawled even more now that Ignacio was gone. Finally Johnny had had enough. Joe had given us too many excuses and runarounds. Johnny called in Sergio to replace Ignacio. Sergio, or Serg, pronounced like "surge," was a tough guy. Scratch that. Sergio was one of the toughest guys in West Liberty's storied history of tough guys. If life were a movie, when Serg walked into a room, there would be a Quentin Tarantino sting and credit accompanying him. *Inglorious Cabrones.*

Johnny and Serg used to deal with the West Liberty of the late '80s and early '90s, where the tensions and racism manifested themselves in more violent ways. By the time their younger brothers went through school, it was a different time. There was still strife and bullshit on the playground, I remember a kid continually referring to my friends and I as "darkies." But it was nothing compared to the stuff that Johnny and Serg used to face. Serg dealt with it head on. The stories of him fighting racist kids towns over were famous in the little-brother circuits. Serg was around less for the roofing and more for the inevitable time Johnny confronted Joe about our wages.

Johnny talked one of the homeowners he was now close with to find the spot where Joe was working with one of his other teams. It was in a run-down neighborhood in Cedar Rapids. We pulled up early in the morning, to catch Joe not too far down in the drink. Our whole squad pulled up minus Darren. However down for the cause Darren was on the rooftops, he confided to us that this wasn't his fight. Johnny's plan was to confront Joe heavy, with Serg and Malcolm behind him as the muscle. Tony, Mark, and I were a little too small, but we could fit the profile in certain people's eyes.

As we walked toward the house, we saw Joe and his unkempt hair on the roof, watching all the other workers.

Malcolm was the first to say it. "Would you look at that. He got himself a team of brothers down here?" I looked over at the workers Joe was overseeing and saw that they were all black. Looking closer I saw they had the same configuration we had on our team, two guys on nail guns, three to four grunts to tear down. Johnny yelled at Joe to come down the ladder. The workers on the roof stopped and watched as Joe came down the ladder. His boots clanked on the metal of the ladder as he made his way down.

"This is the other team you keep blaming for not paying us?" Johnny asked.

"Look, Johnny, I told you what happened. I tried to get supplies for that big project that we could all work on and things got caught up. It happens all the—"

"Don't say anything about how things happened before, old man," Serg said, cutting Joe off. His words were level and short. A warning. "We're here to tell you how things are going to happen. You're going to pay us. Now."

Joe started to reply before stopping himself. He looked small then. Defeated. He ran his hands through his hair, a nervous tic that caused his hair to stand on end like a blue-collar Einstein.

"Fine. Will you take me to the bank then?" Joe asked in a small voice. Johnny nodded for me to do my duty and chauffeur Joe like old times.

I entered the driver's side of Joe's truck and immediately rolled down the window, as was the tradition. Joe fumbled with the passenger-side door as the empty beer cans rattled around the floor.

"Jesus," I muttered to myself.

We drove to the bank in silence, which was fine by me but must have rubbed Joe the wrong way. "You know I wasn't meaning you all any harm, right?" Joe asked.

"I don't care, man. As long as it's behind us."

"You know what the funny thing is, though? I did spend your money on supplies for a bigger project. That part's true."

"Yeah, but how long ago was that?" I asked.

"Hold up, don't get ahead of me," Joe said before taking a deep breath. "But you know that other team, right? Here's the thing with those black folks. They are always bitching about their money. They came up to me with puffed-up chests weeks before you guys did. What's that say about you?"

My jaw clenched as I stared ahead.

"But that's just the way it works. See, the black guys, they'll always demand payment first. That's just how it works. But you—" Joe pointed at me for emphasis. "You guys. The Mexicans. You'll work and work and rarely ask for the money. Not until way past the point of any other group, that's for damn sure. And that's why I'll always sing your praises. To the Mexicans. To the workers," he said and looked at me, in his smelly truck with no AC. Until I finally looked over and saw he had his hand outstretched for a handshake. I looked at his hand, then at his ruddy face. I listened to his labored breathing as he sat. Waiting. I shook his hand and pulled up to the bank as he got our money from the bank teller.

I hated myself for a long time for that handshake. When I delivered the money, I told Serg about it.

"And you shook his fucking hand?" he said.

"I didn't know what else to do."

"I would've knocked him out."

I couldn't stop thinking about it. About the whole situation. The vileness and inherent racism of pitting the two groups against each other. Of my complacency in shaking his hand to get my money. My cosigning of the operation. After that handshake I couldn't look at our roofing the same. I started skipping days, letting the group work on without me. People called me lazy.

Johnny kept his rhythm. He didn't have time to think about the nuances of the discrimination at hand. He needed to work. After about a week of skipping days, he stopped trying to get me up in the morning. He kept at it. Even when Joe kept trying to shortchange him on projects. Even when the other guys followed suit and quit. He kept on working. Until one day he rushed into our kitchen clutching his arm. My mom screamed at the rivulets of blood formed on Johnny's arm. He had broken it falling off a ladder. He winced at the pain of rolling up his shirt and running water over the wound.

"That's not gonna help. You have to go to the hospital!" my mom said. Over and over. Johnny stood over the sink for a long time. The water ran from the faucet as the three of us stood in the kitchen.

"Fine," he said with his eyes closed. My mom sprang to action, fumbled with her keys.

There were only a couple weeks left of the summer by then. The next morning I woke up early to go to an advising session at Kirkwood. I bumped into my brother on my way to make breakfast. He cursed under his breath in the living room, his nondominant hand clawing at the buttons on his shirt. His right hand hung limp by his side in a cast. His footfalls reverberated off our living room walls in an even beat as he passed by me. Off to work another roof. Alone.

There was a knot in my throat walking to the advising session at Kirkwood. Charlie, the jovial Kirkwood adviser, caught me before the entrance.

"Jesus, it is so good to see you again!" He reached out for a handshake. I looked down at the palm before me. A beat. Ignored.

"Jesus, how are you doing? Did you end up getting any cool jobs over the summer?" he asked with a smile.

His hand stood outstretched. Another beat.

"No. I didn't end up working, actually." I fought back tears and walked past him into the advising session.

⁓

I transferred to the University of Iowa after Kirkwood, without the summer jobs. I graduated from the U of I two years later. With big plans and an impending knee injury that dashed said plans. While recovering from this injury, I ended up working at a day center for individuals with special needs. This was hard work. Physically and emotionally. You don't know hard work until you have to account for the basic daily needs of another person. Where someone actually depends on you to *live*. It changed me. Gave me a whole different perspective on privilege and life. There are stories there, big and small, for another time.

But that is to say that I worked at the day center for almost a decade. I used the skills I learned there to come back full circle to the University of Iowa. To Hancher Auditorium, its grandiose performance hall. I jumped for joy when I got the job. A career. Marrying my love for art with the community skills I acquired at the day center. After orientation, my supervisor gave me my keys to the entire building. Same as the other full-time staff, as equals.

Johnny came to visit with his two boys while I was working one of Hancher's first open-house events. At my time at the day center he parted ways with Joe but continued to work real tough construction and factory jobs. But he also had three kids with a woman who's not around anymore. Now he's a single dad working for his kids. Third shift. Side jobs. Whatever he can work for those kids to get ahead.

He walked up to me at a booth in the auditorium. It was the first I had seen him in a long time. He was studying the lobby as he walked on the bright white tile toward me.

"Finally, man. Finally one of us made it," he said after we hugged, the smell of his cologne reminded me of riding in his car as a kid.

A couple of weeks after that my parents came to visit. Only they got lost and ended up in a random university building. Hancher was a newly constructed building at the time, not accurately reflected on their GPS map. My parents called me from the other building's reception area while I walked from the auditorium. I was trying to orient myself to where they said they were. The sun was warm on my face as I tried to find the building they described. Then I heard another voice on the line. My mom had handed her cell to the receptionist of the other building.

"Hi. I'm here with your parents and I *think* they said you work here?" the voice asked.

"No, no, they're at the wro—" I started to reply.

"So I called over to the custodial staff and couldn't get a hold of anyone. Are you there, or with food services? Or should I direct her to the back dock?"

No joke. I stopped in my tracks. Work is what happens when you honor the jobs that made you who you are, but know that those jobs aren't the only ones that define us. Work is what happens when I hung up on the receptionist and set out to defy her preconceived notions. Work is the sound of a nail gun, cutting through the air. It's even rhythm, a story unto itself. Like I said, it's complicated.

UNA HISTORIA SOBRE EL TRABAJO

Chuy Renteria

Traducción al español de Nieves Martín López, edición de Sergio Maldonado

PERMÍTANME QUE LES HABLE de mi relación con el trabajo. Porque si son mexicanos en Estados Unidos, han de tener una relación con el trabajo. Da igual ser inmigrante de primera, segunda o tercera generación, si no tienes papeles, o si estás en una situación similar; tu relación es compleja. Si eres un mexicano en Estados Unidos, el trabajo no es solo un trabajo. El trabajo es la forma en que te mira la gente si tienes un acento diferente. El trabajo es lo oscura que se te pone la piel cuando trabajas en la construcción. El trabajo es lo que pasa cuando trabajas con un grupo de mexicanos techando la casa de un blanco. Paisas y *coconuts*—hombres de mediana edad sin papeles y jóvenes universitarios que no saben hablar español: todos sobre un mismo techo. Pero para la gente que pasa junto a la casa manejando, somos lo mismo, una masa uniforme que pasa desapercibida. Mexicanos en un techo haciendo el trabajo que los conductores preferirían no hacer.

Uno de mis primeros trabajos fue en un súper, en la sección de productos frescos. Llene la solicitud y me respondieron el mismo día. La conversación comenzó con tecnicismos, disponibilidad y contactos, pero viró cuando la encargada de recursos humanos me preguntó por teléfono si les llamaba por el anuncio. En realidad no; necesitaba un trabajo y por eso apliqué. El anuncio era para personas que supieran inglés y español. No recuerdo si pedían específicamente mexico-estadounidenses, ni siquiera sé si eso es legal, pero es exactamente lo que buscaban. La mujer de recursos humanos me preguntó sin rodeos: "¿Entonces, tú puedes hablarle a nuestros clientes hispanohablantes, sí?"

Si tenemos una relación tensa con el trabajo, entonces la primera generación de mexico-estadounidenses sienten que la cosa se complica aún más por el español. Me explico: puedo entender el español... la mayor parte del tiempo. Diría que entiendo un 80 %. Mis padres me hablan solo en español y yo les respondo con este *spanglish* áspero, accidentado, la mayoría en inglés con unos cuantos "peros" y "comos" salpicados por ahí. Hasta mi esposa me dijo que mi inglés cambia cuando hablo con mis padres: se vuelve más simple y mi acento es más fuerte. No me había dado cuenta hasta que ella me lo dijo. Un ejemplo de cómo respondo a las preguntas de mis padres: "No, *I worked long*... pero, *I didn't know when*. Cuando... eight... como a la ocho. Yeah... yeah. No sé, I don't know."

Cambiar de lenguas para mí es como fallar un tiro. Como un botón que se queda encajado y reproduce una y otra vez la misma acción. Pero puedo entender un 80-85 % de lo que me dicen mis padres. Esto asombra a los estadounidenses blancos cuando se lo explico.

—Sí, mi hermano habla español con fluidez. Su hijo mayor no quiere hablar español, pero su hijo pequeño sí. Los hijos de mi hermana no saben hablarlo, aunque ella sea la más mexicana de todos nosotros.

Eso es algo que nos preguntamos, ¿qué tan mexicano eres realmente? Ese sentimiento me pasaba por la cabeza cuando la mujer de recursos humanos me hizo esa simple pregunta, si yo hablaba español o no. Tartamudeé. "Bueno... Sí, entiendo español. Pero no sé qué tan bien puedo hablar sobre frutas y verduras en español." Una vez aprendí con Duolingo que *carrot* en español se dice "zanahoria." Una semana después mi tía la usó en una frase y la coincidencia me volvió loco. Intenté explicarle a la mujer de recursos humanos mi porcentaje de 80 % de comprensión y mi expresión *not-so-good* en español. Ella me dio una charla al estilo de los de recursos humanos para decirme, al final, que a ellos les bastaba.

Después de conseguir el trabajo, mi supervisor me pidió posar para unas fotos que necesitaban para sus anuncios, los de los cupones semanales que la tienda envía los domingos. "¿Por qué no?", me dije, y posé con las naranjas sonriendo a la cámara y diciendo *Cheese!* Unas semanas después, mi amigo Pepe me contó la noticia.

—Oye, te vi en el periódico el otro día por lo de tu trabajo —me dijo.

—¡Oh, sí! ¡Me olvidé de las fotos! ¿Qué tal quedaron? —pregunté.

—Están bien. Se te ve muy gracioso, posando, diciendo cosas que tú nunca dirías.

—¿El qué? ¿Sobre el producto?

—Eso también, pero quería decir el hecho de que te pusieron hablando español, ¡como si de verdad supieras hablarlo!

Corrí lo más rápido que pude a mi casa. Abrí el periódico con ansiedad, buscando el anuncio. Allí estaba: yo, con una naranja en mano, y unos bloques de texto bien grandes en español, puestos en un espacio en blanco sobre mi cabeza. Palabras escritas que apenas entendía, y que mucho menos sabría usar en una conversación fluida; algo sobre la alta calidad del producto. Algo diciendo que si alguna vez necesita ayuda, puede buscar a alguien que se vea como yo, guiño, guiño. "¡Chingado!," pensé. La mamá de mi novia, que es blanca, pensó que yo me veía genial en el anuncio y lo puso en el refrigerador. Mi mamá no pensó lo mismo.

En realidad sí tuve un par de encuentros con hispanohablantes en los pasillos del súper, algunos más exitosos que otros. Ya lo dije, puedo entender español bastante bien, y el nivel del discurso es bastante básico cuando hablas con alguien de temas como el precio de los jalapeños. Una vez la cagué con una mexicana. Me preguntó sobre un descuento de comida enlatada, y mi spanglish salió bien fuerte. Juro por mi vida que no podía recordar la palabra en español para decir fifty, cincuenta. En vez de decir "No, no, esto son cincuenta centavos menos", le dije algo como *"This is five and zero off. Five and zero...* Cinco y cero *off."* Ella se frustró y me dejó allí en el pasillo, no sin antes preguntarme de dónde era yo y *who my mother was.* Quién es mi madre. "¿Qué tan mexicano eres? ¿Qué tan mexicana es tu madre para haberte criado así?" No me quedé trabajando mucho tiempo allí después de eso.

Luego tuve otra serie de trabajos de verano. Estaba tomando clases en Kirkwood y cada verano me quedaba bien pobre, sin un solo dólar en el bolsillo. Mirando atrás, los trabajos que elegí estuvieron interesantes. Debe ser porque escogí trabajos que eran típicamente para mexicanos. Trabajé de cuidador, también en la parte de atrás de una tienda de ropa, y también como limpiaplatos. En el fondo, tenía un chip en el hombro, como si fuera la versión en mexicano de Matt Damon en *Good Will Hunting,* con el trapeador en la mano. Cada vez que algún blanco venía hacia mí cuando estaba limpiando, me causaba un efecto extraño. Yo asumía que ellos asumían que yo no hablaba inglés. Siempre que me preguntaban algo, era innecesariamente extenso en mis explicaciones, como un niño que acaba de descubrir un tesauro. No estoy seguro si la gente lo notaba, o si me notaban a mí siquiera. Denle un trapeador a un mexicano y verán cómo desaparece delante de sus ojos. Además, cuando alguien pregunta por el baño, suele apurarse y alejarse hacia la dirección que le indicas.

Debo tener cuidado con la forma en que hablo de estos trabajos, pues eran duros, y aprendí mucho de ellos. Todavía hoy digo que limpiar y hacer el trabajo que otros no quieren es honroso. El trabajo manual produce una catarsis y un orgullo que ningún trabajo de oficina puede igualar. En *Anna Karenina,* hay una sección en la que se habla con mucho detalle sobre el trabajo en el campo de uno de los personajes. He oído a gente quejarse de lo aburrida que es esta sección, pero a mí casi me arranca las lágrimas. Como dije anteriormente, tenemos una relación complicada con el trabajo.

Hay una historia muy buena del tiempo que pasé en el departamento de ropa. El trabajo me llegó gracias a un asunto familiar. Mi madre consiguió el trabajo primero y nos avisó a mí y a mi hermano Johnny. Pronto convencimos a mi primo Gable para unirse al grupo. La ropa llegaba en grandes camiones a la parte trasera del almacén, la descargábamos, la colgábamos en colgaderos industriales amarillos con ruedas, y luego la llevábamos para clasificarlas en distintos departamentos. Las ruedas del colgadero chirriaban mientras lo arrastrábamos bajo las luces fluorescentes. Todo era muy simple y liberador; la mayor parte del tiempo nos dejaban en paz. Nuestro supervisor era un poco inútil, seguro que un marginado del resto del departamento, pero seguía siendo nuestro jefe. Después, él siempre mencionará la historia que voy a contar bajo el nombre de "el incidente."

El incidente ocurrió así: era cerca del final del día y yo era el último atrás del almacén. Estaba limpiando un poco, metiendo cartón en su conducto, cuando una asociada de ventas entró casi dando un portazo.

—¿Qué está ocurriendo aquí? ¡Estuve intentando llamarlos a "ustedes" durante quince minutos y la línea estuvo ocupada todo este tiempo! —dijo.

Yo eché un vistazo al teléfono color amarillo vivo que estaba en el muro del almacén, el que usaban los asociados de ventas para llamarnos cuando querían que les lleváramos colgaderos. Al mirar el teléfono, veo que está ligeramente descolgado. Me pregunto quién habrá sido la última persona en usarlo, ¿fue Gable, quizás mi ma...?

—¿Hola? —la asociada interrumpió el hilo de mis pensamientos—. ¿Y son "ustedes" son los que están aquí atrás? ¿Escondiéndose para no ayudarnos? ¿Pero qué estoy diciendo? ¿Tan siquiera entiende el inglés?"

Eso fue todo. Esa fue la pregunta. Me gustaría decir que dije lo siguiente. Honestamente no lo recuerdo, pero ojalá, ojalá le hubiera dicho esto: *Yes. I can understand English, I can probably speak it better than you.* "Sí. Entiendo el inglés, y probablemente lo hablo mejor que usted." Mi memoria me falla. Pensando de nuevo en este recuerdo, fantasear con lo que podría haber dicho enturbia las cosas, lo que en verdad dije o no. Es una de las muchas memorias de ducha. Las memorias que de repente te golpean en la ducha, para recordar y recrear las escenas entre el vapor.

"Y aunque no entendiera el inglés, ¡sé lo suficiente para no ser tan grosero como usted!", otra de las respuestas que recreo. Sé que eso no lo dije. Lo que sí dije fue:

—Sí, hablo inglés... Lo siento mucho, no escuché el teléfono —mientras ella agarraba el colgadero y se lo llevaba del almacén.

Recuerdo sentirme indefenso, tanto como cuando llegué a la escuela elemental y era demasiado tímido para hablar. ¿Conocen el juego "Dos verdades y una mentira"? Mi amigo Rubén lo llama un "juego de salón". Tienes que contar dos verdades y una mentira para intentar confundir a la gente. Una de mis verdades favoritas para sorprender al resto es:

—Cuando llegué a la escuela elemental por primera vez, no sabía nada de inglés y solo hablaba con mis padres en español.

Conté esto en mi clase de español avanzado en la universidad, de la que intenté librarme con los exámenes CLEP, pero que tuve que tomar igualmente para cumplir con los requisitos de lengua extranjera. Cuando les conté esa verdad, no se la creyeron. Ellos ya estaban familiarizados con mi *spanglish*, con mi cara roja cada vez que conjugaba los verbos; era imposible que esa fuera la mentira. Yo aún no sé si era cierto o no; es lo que me dijeron mis padres. Creo que tenía más que ver con mi timidez, pero sea como sea recuerdo llegar a la clase de ESL, inglés como segunda lengua, y acabar llorando.

Eso me lleva de nuevo al "incidente." El incidente no fue ese intercambio de palabras, sino la carta al más puro estilo de Steinbeck que escribí después. Cuando esa mujer agarró el colgadero y se lo llevó airada, yo tomé esa indefensión y busqué el cuaderno y lapicero más cercanos. Ese era mi momento a lo *Good Will Hunting*, mi versión mexicana de esa línea, *"How 'bout dem apples?"* Escribí en la hoja ese encuentro, incluyendo la parte de *"Do you even understand English? ¿Tan* siquiera entiende el inglés?", y hablé de lo mucho que aguantábamos los trabajadores de almacén. Hablé de volver a estudiar en un colegio, hablé de la igualdad. Me dejé llevar. Firmé la carta con mi nombre completo, fui al despacho de la gestora jefa de toda la tienda y pasé la carta bajo su puerta. Una semana después, recursos humanos amonestó a la asociada con un par de días libres para reflexionar sobre sus acciones. Mi madre aún recuerda el incidente; ni ella ni el resto de mi familia podían dejar de hablar de ello.

—¡Eso es! Necesitaban escuchar eso para que sepan que somos seres humanos —decía mi madre.

Escribí otra carta un par de semanas más tarde, esta dirigida al jefe de almacén, para hacerle saber que iba a dejar el trabajo definitivamente.

Estos trabajos de verano e incidentes nos dan una idea de mi relación con el trabajo. Trabajar significa algo distinto para los que estamos aquí: es complicado. Nos revela cosas sobre cómo te ves a ti mismo y cómo sientes que otros te ven. Hay un trabajo que condensa esta sensación: techar casas con mi hermano.

Era el verano después de la chamba en el departamento de ropa, tras otro año de clases en ese colegio que tanto odiaba. Yo era un estudiante medio en la escuela secundaria y mis notas no eran tan buenas como para entrar en una universidad de prestigio. Mis buenos amigos fueron a la Universidad de Iowa, uno con una beca de luchador, el otro gracias únicamente a sus logros académicos. Veía el colegio como una carga por no haberme tomado la escuela secundaria tan en serio como debía, lo cual no quiere decir que lo fuera a intentar con más ganas en Kirkwood. Me tomó cuatro años y medio sacarme un diploma asociado que normalmente se consigue en dos. Una vez escuché a mi madre presumiendo frente a los vecinos de que yo había estado en el colegio por X años. Para ella, cuanto más tiempo estuvieras en el colegio, mejor. Los médicos se pasan muchos años en la universidad, ¿cierto? Ni mis vecinos ni yo tuvimos el valor para decirle a mi mamá que la carga de trabajo de un médico no era comparable a cuando yo reprobé álgebra por segunda vez.

Siempre me gustó acabar el curso en primavera y volver a los *hobbies* y la libertad del verano. Ya cerca del fin de semestre, Charlie, uno de los asesores académicos de Kirkwood, me encontró en una sala común. Charlie era una de las mejores personas que he conocido nunca. Un tipo alto con lentes, que siempre estaba al borde de una sonrisa genuina. Lo único que debías hacer era darle una razón para hacerlo. Cuéntale sobre tu día, sobre la carrera que quieres elegir, y él te dará una palmadita cariñosa en el hombro y le saldrá esa sonrisa. Charlie, con trajes de chaqueta con hombreras, solía pasar los descansos del almuerzo en la sala común, y usaba esa hora para ponerse al día con todos los estudiantes que podía. Siempre se acordaba de mi nombre, incluso hace poco, después de casi una década sin verme. Resulta que él era el que convocaba los encuentros de atletismo en mi escuela secundaria.

—¿Cómo iba a olvidar un nombre como el tuyo, *Hey-zeus?* —me dijo.

Volviendo a la historia, Charlie vino a hablar conmigo a la sala común, y me preguntó cómo me iba y si tenía planes para el verano. Le contesté que iba a ser un verano tranquilo, pero que normalmente trataba de encontrar una chamba para tener dinero extra.

—Por supuesto, uno tiene que ganarse el pan, ¿cierto? Pues déjame saber cómo te va, ¡y en qué aventuras te metes! —exclamó Charlie con una carcajada, y me dio una palmadita en el hombro.

Estaba pensando en la pregunta de Charlie sobre mis planes de verano cuando encontré una oferta de trabajo en internet. Todo indicaba ser un puesto de asociado de ventas. Cuando entré a las oficinas, ya era demasiado tarde para echarme atrás; era uno de esos complots piramidales en los que te intentan convencer de que les vendas cuchillos a tus amigos y familiares. La primera reunión de información era para intentar convencernos de comprar el juego de cuchillos para poder comprender mejor el producto; tendríamos que pagar por los cuchillos y entrenar para usarlos. Por supuesto.

Le conté todo a mi mamá y ella se echó a reír y me dijo que era un pendejo. La recepcionista de la empresa me llamó todos los días durante tres semanas para mi primera "entrevista." *Ellos* eran los que me llamaban a mí, y no al contrario, por eso se sabe que era una estafa. Después de reírse, mi mamá concluyó que lo mejor para mí sería trabajar techando casas con mi hermano Johnny, que acababa de volver de Texas y tenía la chamba arreglada. Debía hablar con él. A la mañana siguiente, Johnny me despertó a las seis de la mañana para mi primer día.

Todavía me quedaba sueño en los ojos mientras él manejaba su grandísimo Ford F-150 por la autopista. La casa a la que íbamos estaba a unos 45 minutos de West Liberty, nuestro hogar. Mi hermano es diez años mayor que yo, y por entonces él tenía casi treinta, que es más o menos la misma edad que tengo yo ahora.

Hombre, cuando yo era niño adoraba a Johnny. Él me llevaba a la escuela en su carro, un Firebird negro, con la música de Rage Against the Machine a todo volumen mientras llegábamos a mi escuela primaria. Pensaba que era lo más chido del mundo. Zach de la Rocha es otro mexicano de los nuestros, atrapado en el medio. Tiempo después, Johnny o uno de sus amigos se puso bien pedo y estrelló ese Firebird. Nunca supe todos los detalles de la historia.

A Johnny lo pescaron con demasiadas drogas en su apartamento un par de años antes de nuestro verano techando casas. Por aquel entonces manejó hasta Odessa, Texas, para trabajar en los campos de petróleo con mi tío y desaparecer del mapa por un tiempo. El show adolescente *Friday Night Lights,* sobre un equipo de fútbol americano en la escuela secundaria, tiene lugar en una Odessa ficticia, aunque mis tíos me contaron que todos los mexicanos allí van a la escuela más pobre y el equipo de fútbol americano es una mierda.

Así que Johnny volvió a casa en Navidad ese año. La policía detuvo su carro por llevar una placa de otro estado, y cuando vieron que tenía una orden de arresto, lo encerraron en la prisión local por unos meses. Lo recuerdo saliendo por la puerta la noche que lo dejaron libre, con los ojos vidriosos y una barba desaliñada que nunca había tenido ni tendría después. Ya estaba fuera, pero atrapado en Iowa, pendiente de la vista en el juzgado y buscando trabajo. Él y yo lo encontraríamos juntos. Pero claro, él no me contó nada de esto. Nuestra familia coexiste entre las fracturas de la comunicación, pausas grandes como embarazos mientras pensamos en cosas menos personales que decir.

Normalmente el tema de conversación menos personal es el trabajo que tenemos por delante, y mientras manejábamos por la autopista, eso hicimos.

—Muy bien, pues te cuento. Conocí a este güey, ¿sabes? Un viejo blanco, grandote. Él maneja unos cuantos equipos de obreros, hace techados, enlucidos, y todo eso. Se llama Joe, y el güey antes era un pez gordo. Ahora se perdió en la botella, demasiada bebida. Ya lo verás. Va de aquí para allá como un pollo sin cabeza —me contó Johnny. Recuerdo esa última frase, lo perfecta que era para caracterizar a Joe—. Y nuestro plan es este: mientras el güey este se dedica a hacer el pendejo con sus equipos, nosotros iremos allí a hacer nuestro trabajo. El güey no sabe lo rápido que podemos terminarlo. Aquí hay varo, solo tenemos que trabajar bien y agarrarlo —continuó.

Mi hermano planteaba su jugada como si fuera un maléfico plan. Yo no entendía por qué hacer el trabajo mejor de lo que Joe anticipaba podía ser algo para ocultar, pero es cierto que nunca había visto a mi hermano trabajar. Cuando trabajas más rápido, más duro y mejor de lo que esperan todos, encuentras maneras de superar a tus superiores. Cuando el trabajo es algo tan irregular como los trabajos en la construcción, techando casas, tienes que encontrar la forma de sacar varo sin que lo sepa tu ebrio supervisor.

—Nos juntamos con los dueños de la casa, dejamos que los contactos previos de Joe nos abran las puertas y dejamos fuera al borracho de Joe.

Techar es bastante simple, al igual que la mayoría de los trabajos de fuerza. Se puede aprender lo esencial de todo el proceso en un día. Agarras a una persona de la calle y la puedes enseñar a desmontar las tejas viejas del techo con una demostración en 30 segundos, como hizo Johnny conmigo esa primera mañana. El proceso es el siguiente: agarras una horqueta o una pala para quitar tejas, subes al techo y arrancas las tablas de abajo arriba. Tienes que empujar y raspar bajo las tejas para alcanzar por debajo de los clavos. Entonces haces palanca con la pala y arrancas las tejas. Cuanto más practiques, antes podrás desmontar las tejas en pedazos mayores. Se empieza en el fondo del techo y se trabaja hacia arriba. Es un trabajo monótono, necesario y agotador. Después de quitar las tejas, hay que arrojar los escombros a una lona o contenedor de basura que hay debajo. Cuando pasamos a quitar el fieltro bajo las tablas, entra en juego la delicadeza. Las capas de un tejado, de la más superficial a la más profunda, son las tablas, el fieltro y el triplay. El fieltro está para impermeabilizar la casa. Si se daña el fieltro anterior antes de poner un rollo de fieltro nuevo, podría ser un problema, especialmente si no se tiene un rollo nuevo a mano y hay posibilidad de lluvia. Y luego vienen los regaños por no tener cuidado al arrancar el fieltro y desmontarlo bien.

Después de desmontar todo, hay que subir los nuevos paquetes de tejas al techo. Algunos usan elevadores mecánicos para subir decenas de paquetes de tejas de una sola vez. Nosotros tuvimos que cargar esos paquetes de 80 libras a hombros y subirlos por la escalera. Hacíamos competiciones: a ver quién subía la escalera con más agilidad o a ver quién cargaba más paquetes en un día.

Mi hermano me enseñó lo básico sobre tejados de apartamentos prefabricados en North Liberty. Luego de un par de semanas, empezamos a juntar un grupo de marginados para llevar a cabo el plan de Johnny. Yo convencí a mis primos Tony y Mark para que se unieran. Los dos son un año menores que yo y miembros en mi equipo de baile break. Los tres nos volvimos inseparables ese verano, así lo más lógico era que se juntaran con nosotros y ganaran también algo de dinero. Tony y Mark eran tan primos míos como casi todo el resto de West Liberty. En otras palabras, no éramos primos de verdad; pero oigan, allá en alguna parte de los árboles familiares, una de las tías de mi madre es media hermana de uno de los primos de los padres de ellos dos. Pero para simplificar, éramos mejores amigos que decían ser primos, porque era más fácil decir eso que buscar en las raíces enmarañadas de nuestros árboles familiares. Tony y Mark habían salido de la escuela secundaria, siempre discutiendo o haciendo bromas, y tan perdidos en el mundo real como yo. Éramos peones olvidados, demasiado jóvenes para darnos cuenta de lo malo que era eso.

Una mañana, en la camioneta que nos recogía a todos, Johnny dijo que iba a pasar por Malcolm, uno de sus viejos amigos. Cuando la F-150 estacionó en ese apartamento de Iowa City, Mark fue el primero en reconocer su cara.

—Hombre, ¡pero si es James Truth! —dijo al salir del carro para saludar a Malcolm/James.

—¿Así es como lo conocen ahora? —le preguntó Johnny mientras Tony se unía a Mark para chocar nudillos con James.

James Truth era el nombre artístico de Malcolm, el amigo que Johnny conoció en Iowa City antes de su arresto. En el circuito del hip-hop conocíamos a James Truth. Todos formábamos parte de un espectáculo mensual de hip-hop. James rapeaba y nuestro grupo hacía break en los intermedios. James era de piel oscura, atractivo, tenía mucha labia y era un artista bastante bueno. Intentaba seguir los pasos de los grandes raperos de la época, como 50 Cent o The Game.

—No me importa su nombre, mientras que sepa usar la pistola de clavos— dijo Johnny antes de que el trío se trepara en la camioneta.

Resultó que Malcolm sí sabía manejar la pistola de clavos y clavar tejas. No tan bien como Johnny, pero lo suficiente como para formar parte del equipo. Lo que separa a los simples peones de los techadores habilidosos está en la forma de colocar el fieltro y cuando hay que poner nuevas tejas. Los habilidosos pueden colocar las tejas en su sitio y clavarlas con rapidez. Se puede juzgar la habilidad de un obrero con la pistola de clavos por el sonido rítmico de los clavos al colocar cada tabla y su frecuencia.

Malcolm era bueno: su pistola de clavos hacía un sonido constante y estable, pum... pum... pum, antes de colocar la siguiente tabla y repetir el proceso. Por otra parte, Johnny era un maestro. Alineaba todas las tablas en una fila e iba cambiando de postura sobre sus rodillas con comodidad. Pumpumpumpum-pumpumpumpum-pumpumpumpum —así por todo el tejado. Johnny y Malcolm llevaban viejos almohadones de sofá para apoyar las piernas mientras clavaban las tablas. Si te querías lucir podrías conseguir unas rodilleras, pero nosotros pasábamos con lo que podíamos.

Johnny y Malcolm recordaban viejos tiempos entre disparos de clavos. Tony, Mark y yo nos secábamos el sudor y el polvo de la cara y planeábamos nuestra próxima aventura para el fin de semana. Todos teníamos callos y magulladuras de subir los paquetes de tejas a mano, cortes y raspaduras de tropezar con clavos y escombros. El olor a alquitrán y polvo nos llenaba las fosas nasales mientras trabajábamos bajo el calor abrasador. Hacíamos bromas a costa unos de otros y nos pagaban cada cierto tiempo. El plan de Johnny parecía estar casi completo. El borracho de Joe nos encargaba otro tejado y nosotros lo terminábamos dentro del tiempo estimado o incluso antes, y así una y otra vez.

Por supuesto, nos pagaban en efectivo. No había formularios W2, ni seguro médico, ni impuestos sobre el tipo de trabajo que hacíamos. Los cheques eran rollos de billetes transferidos desde la cuenta bancaria de Joe hasta la mano de Johnny, quien luego dividía la suma entre todo el equipo. Recuerdo mi primera paga, y quiero decir que fue la primera de verdad. No era como los cheques que me daban en el súper, de 7 dólares la hora por trabajar 15 horas a la semana; la primera vez que me pagaron por techar casas, Johnny me dio la mayor cantidad de dinero que jamás había tenido en la mano. Tony, Mark y yo lo gastamos como niños que viven con sus padres y trabajan durante el verano: en videojuegos, ropa, películas y otras cosas que queríamos pero no necesitábamos.

Mi hermano iba ahorrando el dinero. En ese momento no lo pensé mucho, pero tenía que haber adivinado la intención tras el plan de Johnny desde el principio. Mis primos y yo solo disfrutábamos de ese dinero que nos sobraba, pero mi hermano lo necesitaba de verdad. Para las facturas, para los abogados, y para salir cuanto antes de Iowa y continuar con su vida. Ahora pienso en el ritmo de su pistola de clavos y oigo su ansia por intentar salir adelante. Pumpumpum-pumpumpum.

Y al principio lo estábamos consiguiendo, ir por delante de todo, del calendario, acabando los trabajos antes de que Joe pudiera conseguirnos otro. Estábamos ganando mucho dinero. Incluso Joe nos pagaba mejor porque estaba feliz con nuestro trabajo.

—Ustedes sí son rápidos, no como los otros equipos que tengo —nos decía Joe cada vez que sacaba dinero para nosotros. Normalmente Joe me pedía que lo llevara en carro al banco, pues él empezaba a abrirse latas de Busch Light cerca de las 8 de la mañana. No me importaba ser su chófer, porque eso me permitía alejarme del trabajo manual y acercarme más al dinero.

Esas primeras semanas fueron simples y lo más entretenidas que podían ser, tratándose de trabajo manual. Trabajábamos deprisa y nos recompensaban por ello. Joe casi siempre nos dejaba en paz, menos un par de veces que apareció sujetando una escalera de mano tambaleante para inspeccionar nuestro trabajo. Todos nos pusimos más morenos. Empezamos a notar que las chicas empezaban a notar que nos estábamos poniendo fuertes. Yo odiaba comer demasiado a la hora del almuerzo porque eso hacía más duro el resto del día, así que me limitaba a ensaladas, pollo y agua. Mi dieta y la carga de trabajo me pusieron en buena forma, más que en toda mi vida. Un día, Johnny agarró crema para el sol, y después se la pasó a Malcolm.

—¡Venga ya! No he conocido todavía a un solo negro que haya usado eso en su vida —exclamó Malcolm mientras me pasaba la crema. Me quedé mirando la forma en que los tatuajes de su brazo se camuflaban entre su piel, y luego miré la botella azul en mi mano.

—Yo tampoco lo he usado nunca —dije, y le pasé el bote de nuevo a Johnny.

—¿Estás seguro? ¿No será porque quieres verte cool delante de Malcolm, no?

Pues sí, así era. Recuerdo sorprenderme de la cantidad de crema solar que se ponían mis amigos blancos en la alberca de Kimberly Park. Por su parte, ellos se asombraban de lo moreno que me ponía yo mientras que a ellos les salían manchas rosadas en las partes del cuerpo sin crema.

Tony, Mark y yo nos quitamos las playeras y trabajamos todo el día bajo el sol para tener el mejor bronceado. Al día siguiente, me picaba la espalda al sentarme en el asiento trasero del camión. Empezábamos pronto en la mañana, cuando todavía hacía fresco. Alrededor de las 9 o las 10 ya hacía calor como para quitarnos las sudaderas, y a las 11.30 ya nos estábamos quitando las playeras.

—¿Qué pedo, güey? ¡Tienes toda la espalda quemada! —me dijo Mark al tiempo que llamaba la atención de Tony. Al mirar la espalda de Mark, me di cuenta de inmediato de cómo se veía la mía.

—¡No manches! ¿Y yo me veo tan pendejo como ustedes? —

preguntó Tony antes que yo pudiera hacerlo. Habíamos conseguido quemarnos la espalda por completo, pero al trabajar en el tejado siempre de espaldas al sol, teníamos toda la parte delantera del cuerpo blanca. Parecíamos tres tristes langostas, con la espalda roja y el vientre blanco. Johnny y Malcolm se reían con ganas a nuestra costa en el techo.

Seguimos con el mismo ritmo durante junio y julio. Tumbamos y pusimos techos nuevos en Iowa City, North Liberty, Cedar Rapids y muchos pueblitos del sureste de Iowa. Me enfrenté a mi miedo a las alturas sobre una monstruosidad de techo de tres pisos. Tuvimos que clavar tablas de 2x4 pulgadas al tejado para poder caminar sobre él, porque tenía demasiada inclinación.

Todo iba bien hasta que Joe empezó a notar todo el dinero que estábamos ganando. Así funcionan las cosas; me refiero a que Joe empezó a notarlo como alguien que nota que puede sacar más provecho de otras personas. Las cosas se pusieron tensas cuando Joe empezó a reclutar nuevos miembros para nuestro equipo, y el primero que nos presentó era este güey llamado Darren. De todo el verano que pasé techando casas, Darren fue el único blanco que nos trató como a iguales, es decir, que no se consideraba superior a nosotros de ningún modo y se sentía orgulloso de trabajar a nuestro lado. Era un hombre fibroso de mediana edad que tartamudeaba al hablar, un peón, pero trabajaba duro. A Darren le gustaba hacernos ver lo chingón que era, usando expresiones mexicanas y hablando de los tipos de mujeres que le atraían.

—*It don't matter* güey, *I'll t-talk to any* mami —nos contaba en los descansos, todos sentados al borde del tejado con las piernas colgando en el aire.

Un día nublado en Mt. Vernon, Joe se acercó a nosotros para hablar del último miembro que se iba a unir a nuestro grupo. Los días nublados eran complicados: Johnny siempre estaba nervioso por si se ponía a llover, porque entonces tendríamos que cubrir todas las áreas del tejado sin tablas y dejarlo para el día siguiente. A la mayoría de nosotros no nos importaba tener un día libre, pero para Johnny significaba otro día de retraso en el proyecto. Joe fue hacia Johnny, oliendo a cerveza barata.

—A ver, Johnny, voy a traer un güey que se unirá a nuestro

equipo –dijo Joe. Johnny reprimió una sonrisa al oír lo de "nuestro equipo".

–¿Ah, sí? ¿Esta vez será alguien que sepa manejar de verdad la pistola de clavos? –respondió.

–Claro, claro. Mira, Johnny, este tipo es un ilegal, y ya me conoces, me vale verga si es ilegal o de Marte. Lo único que miro es si trabaja bien–. Johnny dejó la pistola de clavos y se sentó en su almohadón para observar a Joe–. Este güey, Arturo, trabajó conmigo antes, y te puedo decir que es el mejor obrero que he tenido. En un día, podía acabar con un tejado entero él solito–. Johnny se echó a reír.

–Muy bien. No voy a debatirle. ¿Y cuándo empieza?

–Bueno, le explico, Arturo está ocupado con no sé qué mierdas allá en México. De verdad que no sé lo que les pasa a *ustedes los mexicanos,* pero se metió en un lío y no puede venir. Una pena, porque le dije que aquí se puede ganar mucho dinero. Entonces Arturo va a enviar a su hermano para trabajar con nosotros.

–¿Y es bueno? –preguntó Johnny.

–Si es la mitad de buen obrero que Arturo, nos servirá –dijo Joe, pasándose la mano por el cabello alborotado casi canoso, y después escupió un cohete de flema por el tejado.

Una semana más tarde, Ignacio, el hermano de Arturo, se presentó en nuestra casa a las siete de la mañana, dispuesto a trabajar.

–Muy bien, veamos qué sabe hacer este mexicano –me dijo Johnny mientras llenaba su termo con café antes de subirnos a la camioneta. Entonces Johnny relegó a Tony y Mark a la cama de la camioneta, entre pilas de tejas y herramientas, y bromearon al paso del viento.

Resultó que Ignacio en verdad no era ni la mitad de buen obrero que Arturo. Con la pistola de clavos estaba entre el nivel de Malcolm y el de Johnny; no era el maestro pistolero que mi hermano esperaba. Ignacio era el suplente mediocre de sheriff del Cisco Kid de Johnny, pero eso igualaba la proporción entre pistoleros y peones. Malcolm, Johnny e Ignacio clavaban las secciones del tejado que Tony, Mark, Darren y yo desmontábamos.

Johnny hacía de intérprete para Ignacio por todos nosotros. Johnny hablaba el español con soltura y dejó que Ignacio entrara en nuestros planes de verano. En este punto íbamos bastante adelantados a la fecha de los proyectos asignados. Un día vi que Johnny avanzó en su jugada con el propietario: primero le preguntó por el proyecto que habíamos terminado y luego le dijo:

—Oiga, si sabe de alguien más que necesite un arreglo, dele mi número.

El propietario pensó entonces que Johnny era el único que realmente quería las chambas.

—Sí, ¿sabe que Joe antes era un hombre respetable? Ahora está demasiado metido en la bebida. En el fondo ese güey sigue ahí... ¿Podría repetirme su número?

Johnny le dio el número, y luego estrecharon las manos cordialmente.

Muy pronto ya sumábamos otros proyectos de los que Joe no estaba al tanto. Johnny nos dividió, tres trabajando aquí y los otros cuatro allí ese día. Los de allí se estaban haciendo de oro. Aunque Ignacio no era como su famoso hermano Arturo, nos bastaba para acelerar el proceso. El grupo empezó a sintonizar en conjunto. Eso, hasta que nos tocó esa casa en West Liberty. Era una casa nueva en obras, y eso debería haber puesto las cosas más fáciles, incluso Johnny había ido a la misma escuela secundaria que el propietario de la casa.

—¡Qué sorpresa! ¡Nunca pensé que tú serías uno de los que trabajara en mi nueva casa! —exclamó el güey el primer día que nuestro pintoresco grupo entró a su propiedad.

La casa tenía algo que traía mala suerte. Tony y Mark empezaron a mencionar la palabra "maldita". La llamaban "la casa de la colina," como en *House on the Hill*. Estuvo lloviendo a ratos en nuestra primera semana. Las tejas que Johnny había traído en un palé se habían podrido y eran inservibles. Hubo una gran cantidad de accidentes en ese sitio. Comenzamos a retrasarnos en nuestros planes.

La casa de la colina se perfilaba con toda la integridad estadounidense por fuera, pero el interior era lo que nos traía mala suerte, sobre todo por las chapuzas baratas en la construcción para intentar ahorrar dinero. Johnny señaló algunas de ellas.

—No puedo creer lo que veo. Miren eso. El güey está tratando de ahorrarse los pesos haciendo chapuzas, y quiere que se vea bonito.

¿Y por qué no hacer bien el trabajo desde el principio?

Para ser honesto, yo no me di cuenta de algunas cosas que señalaba. Ese verano comprendí las diferencias fundamentales entre nosotros. En lo que a techar se refiere, Johnny sentía un orgullo intenso por su trabajo y por el resultado final. Solía criticar los tejados mal hechos que pasábamos por la calle, o comentar que él los podría haber hecho de una forma más simple y efectiva. Nos pedía que dibujáramos de nuevo las líneas de tiza que habíamos puesto en el fieltro del tejado, una y otra vez, hasta que estuvieran perfectas. A veces me sentía en el set de filmación de una película de Stanley Kubrick, con esa atención a los detalles tan exagerada. Me imagino la situación: las tomas en el set de *2001*, con Stanley haciendo que los simios carguen tejas por la escalera "correctamente."

La única vez que Johnny le dejó la pistola de clavos a los tres primos, uno de nosotros colocó una teja torcida y clavó un tornillo de más. Aunque fue en una parte del tejado que ningún propietario veía, Johnny nos hizo desmontar toda esa fila de tejas y colocar una nueva en perfecta posición.

—Tenemos que demostrar que podemos hacer esto bien. Estén orgullosos de su trabajo —decía, a nosotros y a él mismo.

El día que me electrocuté con un cable descubierto, tuvimos que dejar el trabajo temprano. No por el accidente, si no porque ya era bien entrado julio y empezaba a hacer mucho calor, ese calor que te hacía ver ondas bailando en el aire; tanto calor que cuando caminábamos sobre el tejado, las botas dejaban huellas de alquitrán sobre las tablas. Al principio Johnny dijo que camináramos arrastrando los pies por el tejado con cuidado, pero cuando Darren y yo dejamos un reguero de huellas bastante notable, Johnny nos pidió que lo dejáramos.

—¡Esto es una mierda, vamos a tener que rehacer todo el tejado! —se quejó Johnny. Mientras bajaba por la escalera, traté de disimular mi cara de resignación.

Los hogares de nueva construcción son diferentes, porque hay varios equipos de obreros trabajando codo con codo. Había un equipo enluciendo la casa, otro echando concreto para la entrada del carro, electricistas, etc. Mi hermano y yo nos intercambiábamos indirectas pasivo-agresivas sobre las huellas del tejado cuando pasamos al lado de una de esos equipos. Eran un grupo de chicos de secundaria enyesando el interior del garaje de la casa. Nos ignoraron al pasar mi hermano y yo junto con nuestros primos. Ser ignorados por otros obreros —qué carajo, por todo el mundo— era muy común, como en mis días de cuidador; casi como que te desvaneces cuando estás trabajando.

Pero los chicos tuvieron otra reacción al ver a Malcolm. Vi cómo uno de ellos le daba un codazo a otro para llamar la atención de nuestro amigo, mientras ellos trataban de sacudirse el yeso pegado a sus playeras y se dirigían a hablar con James Truth.

—*Ay yo man*, ¿tienes un cigarro? —preguntó uno de ellos.

Yo sospechaba que ellos ya sabían que sí. Los dos chicos se quedaron hablando con Malcolm por unos quince minutos. La conversación acabó con uno de los chicos mostrándole algunos raps a Malcolm, que lo observaba y se reía. De camino a la camioneta, al terminar el trabajo porque la temperatura iba subiendo, Johnny le preguntó a Malcolm:

—¿Y a qué vino todo eso?

—Hay que darle al público lo que pide. Me dijeron que irían a mi próximo concierto —contestó él.

Después de algunos percances más, acabamos el encargo bastante atrasados. Estábamos felices de haber terminado y poder seguir con otro, especialmente porque al no haber hecho otros trabajos estábamos más lejos de ir consiguiendo dinero. Empezamos una casa nueva en Iowa City y agarramos buen ritmo. Joe nos solía pagar los viernes, aunque hubiéramos completado antes los encargos. Era su manera de tratar de mantener una sensación de profesionalidad. Ese viernes trabajando en la casa de Iowa City se pasó, y también el siguiente. Estábamos bien entrados en julio sin un peso en el bolsillo del encargo de la casa maldita. Joe no paraba de ponerle excusas a Johnny, hablando de que su otro equipo también reclamaba el dinero y que tenía planeado pagarnos a todos juntos.

Tony y Mark empezaron a hablar más con Ignacio, y le enseñaron palabras en inglés al igual que enseñaron español a Darren. Ignacio les preguntó cómo decir "Págame" en inglés. Mark respondió:

—No, no, si vas a hablar con Joe tienes que decirle: *Fuck you. Pay me.*

Ignacio repitió la frase con su acento bien marcado, las manos estiradas sobre el tejado.

—Ay, pinche Joe. *Fuck you. Pay me.*

Tony, Mark e Ignacio se reían mientras tomaban turnos para reclamar dinero al Joe invisible en el tejado. La pistola de clavos de Johnny cortaba el aire a compases regulares.

Al acabar nuestro último trabajo, y sin vistas de conseguir nuestro dinero, las cosas se pusieron tensas. Incluso Tony y Mark estaban de mal humor, porque dejaron de bromear mientras trabajaban. Estuvimos un par de días trabajando en relativo silencio, con el ruido ambiental de los coches y el canto de los pájaros mezclado con el sonido metálico de nuestras herramientas.

Uno de esos sábados Ignacio ya había tenido suficiente. Vino a nuestra casa por la tarde. Al abrir la puerta frontal, empezó a disparar frases en español rápidamente. Yo no entendí lo que me decía, pero sabía que estaba furioso. Intenté que se calmara hasta que por fin lo hizo y señaló detrás de mí para indicar que le hablaba a mi hermano.

—*Fuck you! Pay me!* —disparó antes de irse de allí disgustado.

Esa noche hablé con mi hermano.

—No dejo de decirle a Ignacio que Joe no para de chingarme. Todos estamos jodidos, él no es el único —me dijo Johnny. Yo me dediqué a observar los videojuegos que había comprado el mes anterior, después cambié de tema.

Después de ese incidente no pasó mucho tiempo hasta que Ignacio dejó el equipo permanentemente. Resulta que él le estaba enviando la mayor parte de su dinero a su hermano para sacarlo de los apuros en México. Con el poco varo que le quedaba, rentaba un apartamento detrás de una lavandería en el centro. Era un closet del lavadero que alguien había convertido en un "estudio." Ignacio enviaba demasiado dinero a su país y por eso no pudo cubrir la renta de agosto, así que lo corrieron de allí y se quedaron con su depósito. Si Kurt Vonnegut fuese mexicano, ¿diría eso de *"So it goes"* o en cambio, "Así pasa"?

Si ya nos costaba mucho trabajar después de la casa maldita, aún nos costó mucho más cuando Ignacio se fue. Y así, Johnny decidió que ya le valía madre. Joe nos había dado demasiadas excusas y rodeos. Johnny llamó a Sergio para ocupar el lugar de Ignacio. Sergio, o Serg (como surge), era un güey bien cabrón. Espera, borremos eso; era uno de los güeyes más cabrones en la historia de todos los cabrones de West Liberty. Si la vida fuera como una película y Serg entrara en un salón, se verían créditos de Quentin Tarantino a un lado de la escena. Inglorious Cabrones.

Johnny y Serg tuvieron que lidiar con el West Liberty de finales de los ochentas y principios de los noventas, en que las tensiones y el racismo eran más visibles y se manifestaban de forma violenta. Cuando nosotros, los hermanos pequeños, fuimos a la secundaria, ya eran otros tiempos. Todavía había peleas y otras pendejadas en el patio de la escuela; aún recuerdo al chavo que se refería a mis amigos como *darkies,* los prietos. Pero eso no era nada comparado con lo que Johnny y Serg tuvieron que enfrentar. Serg siempre hacía frente a todos. Sus historias de peleas con los chavos racistas de otros pueblitos se hicieron famosas entre los hermanos menores.

Serg no estaba ahí para techar con nosotros, sino por ese momento ineludible en que Johnny se enfrentó a Joe por nuestros salarios. Johnny le dijo a uno de los propietarios que estaba cerca de averiguar el lugar donde Joe trabajaba con otro de sus equipos. Estaba en un barrio de Cedar Rapids venido a menos.

Estacionamos la camioneta por la mañana temprano, para encontrar a Joe ya casi pedo. Todo nuestro equipo se acercó a hablar con él, menos Darren. Por mucho que nos apoyara arriba en los techos, nos confió que esa no era su bronca. El plan de Johnny era confrontar a Joe de una, con Serg y Malcolm como el músculo para soportar nuestros argumentos. Tony, Mark y yo teníamos poco músculo, pero a ojos de algunos podríamos pasar por chingones. De camino a la casa, vi a Joe y su cabello despeinado sobre el tejado, observando a los otros obreros. Malcolm fue el primero en decirlo:

—Miren eso. ¿Así que tiene otro equipo trabajando aquí?

Eché un ojo a los obreros que Joe supervisaba y vi que eran todos negros. Al prestar más atención vi que tenían la misma organización que nuestro equipo: dos muchachos con pistola de clavos y tres peones para desmontar las tejas viejas. Johnny le gritó a Joe que bajara de ahí. Los obreros dejaron de trabajar mientras nos observaban. Las botas de Joe chocaban con la escalera al bajar y hacían un ruido metálico.

—¿Este es el otro equipo al que culpas de no pagarnos? —preguntó Johnny.

—Mira, Johnny, ya te dije lo que pasó. Traté de conseguir suministros para el gran proyecto en el que íbamos a trabajar todos, pero las cosas se complicaron. Esto pasa todo el—

—No nos hable de las cosas del pasado, viejo —le cortó Serg. Sus palabras eran breves y directas, en forma de advertencia—. Vinimos para decirle lo que va a pasar a partir de ahora. Nos va a pagar lo que nos debe, ahora mismo.

Joe intentó responder, pero se frenó. Se veía muy pequeño, derrotado. Se pasaba las manos por el cabello, un tic nervioso que hacía que se le parara el pelo como a un Einstein azul.

—Como digan. ¿Me acercan al banco entonces? —preguntó Joe en voz baja. Johnny me hizo una señal para que cumpliera con mi deber de chófer, como en los viejos tiempos.

Subí al carro por la parte del conductor y bajé las ventanillas de inmediato, como ya era tradición. Joe intentó abrir la puerta del copiloto con torpeza, y las latas de cerveza en el piso repiquetearon.

—¡Ay, Jesús! —murmuré.

Manejamos al banco en silencio. A mí no me importaba, pero a Joe le debió caer mal.

—¿Sabes que yo no quería causarles problemas, verdad? —me preguntó.

—No me importa, hombre. Queremos dejar eso atrás.

—¿Pero sabes lo gracioso? Que sí gasté su dinero en suministros para ese gran proyecto, eso era cierto.

—Ya, ¿y cuánto tiempo hace de eso? —pregunté.

—Espera, no te me adelantes —respondió Joe. Después respiró hondo y continuó—: ¿Viste al otro equipo de peones? Pues lo que pasa con los negros es que siempre se están quejando y pidiendo dinero. Ellos vinieron a mí, sacando pecho, antes que ustedes. ¿Y qué dice eso de ustedes los mexicanos? —Yo apreté la mandíbula mientras manejaba sin mirarlo—. Que así funciona el mundo. Mire, los negros siempre quieren que se les pague primero, es así. Pero usted —y me señaló a mí para enfatizar— ustedes, los mexicanos, trabajan y trabajan, pero casi nunca reclaman dinero. Ningún otro grupo aguanta callado tanto tiempo, eso seguro. Y por eso siempre diré cosas buenas de los mexicanos, esos peones.

Joe me miraba, los dos en su camioneta sin aire acondicionado, hasta que por fin decidí mirarle de reojo. Vi que tenía la mano estirada para que se la saludara. Mi mirada pasó de su mano a su cara rojiza. Podía oír su respiración dificultosa ahí sentado. Esperando. Le saludé la mano y estacioné la camioneta para que él fuera por el dinero a su banco.

Me odié a mí mismo durante mucho tiempo por aquel apretón de manos. Cuando entregué el dinero a mi equipo, le hablé a Serg de lo que había ocurrido.

—¿Y le saludaste su pinche mano? —me preguntó.

—No sabía qué otra cosa hacer.

—Yo le habría reventado el hocico.

No podía parar de pensar en todo aquello, en la situación. En el racismo inherente y vil de enfrentar a los dos grupos, en mi complacencia al saludarle la mano para conseguir mi dinero. Yo era cómplice en esa operación. Después de aquel apretón de manos ya no pude ver nuestro trabajo de techadores del mismo modo. Comencé a faltar días de trabajo y dejé que el grupo fuera sin mí. Me empezaron a llamar flojo.

Johnny siguió su ritmo; él no tenía tiempo para pensar en los matices discriminatorios de la tarea, solo necesitaba el trabajo. Tras una semana sin trabajar, Johnny dejó de llamarme para irme con ellos por la mañana. Él siguió a la suya, aun cuando Joe trataba de acortar el plazo de los proyectos, aun cuando los demás dejaron el trabajo. Johnny siguió con su plan. Hasta que un día entró en la cocina agarrándose el brazo. Mi madre pegó un grito al ver los ríos de sangre que le brotaban de la herida. Se había roto el brazo al caerse de la escalera. Se retorció de dolor al subirse las mangas de la playera y dejar que el agua limpiara la herida.

—Eso no ayudará. ¡Tienes que ir al hospital! —gritaba mi mamá una y otra vez.

Johnny estuvo parado junto a la pileta durante un buen rato. El agua corría bajo el grifo mientras los tres mirábamos la herida.

—De acuerdo —dijo Johnny con los ojos cerrados.

Mi madre saltó a la acción, buscando las llaves atropelladamente.

Entonces solo quedaban un par de semanas de verano. A la mañana siguiente me levanté temprano para asistir a mi sesión de orientación en Kirkwood.

Me crucé con mi hermano de camino a desayunar. Él maldecía entre dientes desde la sala, agarrando los botones de su camisa con su mano no dominante. Su mano derecha, enyesada, le colgaba sobre el costado. Sus pasos reverberaron en los muros de nuestra sala en un sonido rítmico al pasar por mi lado. Y allá se iba, a techar de nuevo. Él solo.

Yo tenía un nudo en la garganta de camino a mi sesión orientativa en Kirkwood. Charlie, el jovial asesor académico, me detuvo en la entrada.

—Jesús, ¡qué bueno verte aquí de nuevo! —Me tendió la mano. Yo observé la palma ante mí. Una pausa. Lo ignoré—. ¿Jesús, cómo estás? ¿Al final conseguiste algún trabajo chido en verano? —me preguntó con una sonrisa.

Su mano extendida. Otra pausa.

—No. Al final no encontré trabajo.

Luché por contener las lágrimas al dejar a Charlie atrás, y continué hacia la orientación.

∽

Me cambié a la Universidad de Iowa después de Kirkwood, sin buscar trabajos de verano. Me gradué en UI dos años más tarde, con grandes planes y una lesión de rodilla latente que los destrozaría luego. Mientras me recuperaba de esa lesión, estuve trabajando en un centro de día para personas con necesidades especiales. Era un trabajo duro. Física y emocionalmente duro. No sabes lo que es el trabajo duro hasta que tienes que ocuparte de las necesidades diarias de otra persona, hasta que alguien depende de ti para *vivir*. Eso me cambió; me dio otra perspectiva completamente distinta de la vida y nuestros privilegios. De ahí tengo historias, unas más largas y otras más breves, que ya contaré en otro momento.

Pero diré que estuve trabajando en ese centro de día durante casi una década. Usé las habilidades que aprendí allí para completar el ciclo y volver a la Universidad de Iowa, al auditorio Hancher, con su grandioso salón de actuaciones. Salté de alegría cuando me dieron el trabajo. Una carrera que casaría mi amor por el arte con las habilidades de servicio a la comunidad que adquirí en ese centro de día. Después de la orientación, mi supervisor me dio llaves de todo el edificio, como al resto de los empleados a tiempo completo. Como a un igual.

Johnny vino de visita con sus dos chavitos cuando yo estaba trabajando en una de las primeras jornadas de puertas abiertas de Hancher. En la época que yo pasé en el centro de día, él dejó de trabajar con Joe, pero continuó en otras construcciones y fábricas. También tuvo tres hijos con una mujer con la que ya no está. Ahora es un padre soltero que trabaja para sus hijos, con tres turnos al día y encargos ocasionales. Lo que haga falta con tal de que los chavos salgan adelante.

Mi hermano se acercó a la cabina del auditorio. Era la primera vez que lo vi en mucho tiempo. Se dedicó a estudiar el vestíbulo mientras recorría los azulejos blancos hacia mí.

—Por fin, güey. Por fin uno de nosotros lo consiguió —me dijo después de abrazarnos. El olor de su colonia me trajo a la mente esos días cuando yo era niño y él me llevaba a la escuela en su carro.

Un par de semanas más tarde vinieron a verme mis padres, solo que se perdieron y acabaron en un edificio cualquiera de la universidad. Hancher era un edificio recién construido por entonces, así que el GPS no lo reflejaba correctamente. Mis padres me llamaron desde la recepción de ese otro edificio cuando yo salía del auditorio. Estaba intentando orientarme hacia el sitio que me habían descrito. El sol me daba en la cara. Entonces escuché otra voz al otro lado del teléfono; mi madre le había pasado el teléfono a la recepcionista del edificio.

—Hola. Estoy aquí con sus padres y creo que dijeron que usted trabaja aquí... —dijo una voz, casi en tono de pregunta.

—No, no, están en el edificio equivoc...

—Pues llamé a los del servicio de conserjería, pero no he conseguido contactar con nadie. ¿Trabaja con ellos o con los del servicio de comida? ¿O le dirijo a su madre al almacén?

No miento. Me detuve en seco.

El trabajo es lo que ocurre cuando honras los trabajos que te hacen ser quien eres, pero que sepan que esos trabajos no son los únicos que nos definen. El trabajo es lo que ocurre cuando cuelgo la llamada con la recepcionista y me propongo desafiar esas nociones preconcebidas.

El trabajo es el sonido de una pistola de clavos cortando el aire. Es ritmo, es una historia en sí misma. Como les dije, es complicado.

MAIJOMA, MY SISTER

Chuy Renteria

I.

THE VIEWS FROM THE BACKSEAT WINDOW were of scant brush and jagged thistles, passing flora marked by its thirst for rain. My dad was driving the last leg of his homeward journey in silence while my mom napped in the front seat. The city of Ojinaga was in our rearview mirror. The orange trees that lined its streets diminished from sight as my dad drove, its swatches of dust and sepias, like old photographs of relatives, specks in the reflection as we took the highway to my father's hometown. We were driving through the Mexican state of Chihuahua, about an hour from the city of Ojinaga, to the pueblo of Maijoma, pronounced like "My Home Uh."

My skin stuck to the sunlit backseat as I shifted my position. The heat and discomfort made it hard for me to remember, to align the passing landscape with any memories from my childhood. It had been fifteen years since our family last made this trek to Mexico. A twenty-hour drive. Starting from my small hometown of West Liberty, Iowa, through the border city of Ojinaga, and to the even smaller, secluded village my dad grew up in.

Fifteen years ago, my older sister Maria was with me in the backseat. We were leaving a *quinceañera* we attended in Ojinaga for her. It wasn't Maria's *quinceañera* but, with her being fourteen years old, my parents planned it so we would be a part of the ceremony. They hoped she could get a taste of what she would be experiencing in a year's time. That it would excite her. All I remember of the celebration was that, at nine years old, I was too young to be an escort, a *chambelán*. I was happy when the formal pomp of the ceremonies were over and I could run outside the dusty dance hall with the other young boys. Away from the adults drinking and partying. Away from the teenagers playing dress-up. The *bailes* in Ojinaga were the same as the ones in Iowa. Dark and full of bodies. When us kids would open the doors to run outside, cigarette smoke

51

would billow out toward the night sky. I remember brushing sand onto the back seat of the car when the night's festivities were over. From my clothes. From my hair and shoes and onto the car floor. We were heading from the hall to Maijoma in the darkness. A couple years prior my sister would have dominated the rest of us in the muddy games outside the *bailes*. But now she was pristine and dressed up beside me. Her hair all bangs like Selena on *Johnny Canales*. She sat looking outside her car window. Her face coming into and out of the light of the passing street lamps.

It had been fifteen years and my parents were in the front seat driving the same drive from Ojinaga to Maijoma. The sunlight overexposed the views from our car. I was trying to remember. To think about what she could have been thinking. Was it about how when you leave Ojinaga, it feels like you're leaving civilization behind? A road off the highway leads to more and more unserved roads, until it feels like you're driving along paths that don't quite feel tended by any definitive entity but rather forged by the repeated treks of a select people, going to visit family.

It was spring break from college courses and my parents told me, "This could be the last time you see your grandparents before they die. You need to go." It was not the first spring break where they used this reasoning to entice me to visit Maijoma, but it was the first time the reasoning worked.

It had been a while since I'd even hung out with my immediate family, let alone the decade-plus since I'd seen *mis abuelos*. The spring break was a respite from the courses that I was taking. As the first one in my family to attend college, I was not taking the transition well. I wasn't failing or anything like that, but something seemed off. The last couple of times I walked up to the building of one of my classes, I slowed at the entrance. Fighting what I now know as panic attacks. I stood before the entrance, unable to cross, trying to catch my breath as others walked by me unaware.

I was at ease in the back seat of my parent's car in comparison, as I let the worry of school and life dissipate. As I tried to recall my memories. I was thinking of *mis abuelos* and my memories of this place. My dad slowed our car before a makeshift gate. I was thinking of my sister.

We'd been at this gate before, or at least it felt like we had. For all I knew there were thousands of gates like this one dotting Mexico's landscape. Wood posts and barbed wire erected by herders and ranchers, by families like ours. This could have been any other gate, but as my dad got out of the car, he approached it with familiarity. My memory aligned with my dad's confidence in movement. We actually had been here before. The last time we stopped here my *apá* was already at the gate by the time Maria and I got out of the car to meet him.

"Okay, *ayudame*. With this here. *Aquí.* Look," *Apá* said to Maria and me back then, as he pulled at the rotting wood post. We each grabbed part of the post and dragged it away from the fence, the attached barbed wire falling into a netlike mass, scratching a pattern along the dirt. We propped the heap of wood and wire along itself. My mom pulled the station wagon through as we stood under the desert moon and stars.

"*Ya,* let's put it all back up behind us." Our dad said after we got the gate closed, he directed my mom to turn off the side and follow him as walked through the dust.

"We should get some gas here," he said as stepped aside and waved my mom through.

"What are you talking about? There's no gas stations," Maria said as we walked alongside our *apá*. As I looked around, there was only the same desolation we had been driving through since Ojinaga. No signs of a gas station, no buildings or people of any kind. My mom laughed at our confusion as she got out of the car. My dad walked over and knelt down at a random spot with the same intent he had shown at the gate. He pulled at a hose emanating from the ground.

"Yeah, it's still here. They still got it," he said to himself. He put his mouth around the hose until he spit out what looked like oil. The dark fluid poured from the hose as my dad beckoned for Maria to bring a gas can closer. On the transition, the fluid splashed and soiled Maria's shirt as we laughed. This felt like a secret treasure, an X marked on a map somewhere, for families to show themselves as they drove through the isolation. After my dad finished filling the gas can, it began to rain. Big, fat drops that stung with cold.

"Bet I can beat you to the gate and back. Bet," I said to Maria, already limbering up for the race. Maria, having used the rain to wring out the oil from her shirt, was trying to cover her hair. She hadn't yet realized it was a lost cause.

"Nah, I'm good," she replied, distracted.

"What, you think you can still beat me? Not anymore," I said to her as I skipped away, gaining a head start. Maria looked up at the sky as the rain picked up. The drops of water left streaks across the makeup on her face.

"Alright then. Go!" she said as she started to sprint and closed the gap between us. We ran through the rain, kicking up dirt and mud. Since that time, I can never remember another instance of us running full sprint together. I was happy then, in that moment. We both were.

"Ay, Angel! *¿Vas a ayuda to apá or no?* You gonna help!?" my mom said, snapping me from my memories.

"Oh! Oh, yeah. Sorry." I got out to help my dad, who was already halfway through unwinding the gate. As I walked closer, I reflected at how similar it all was. Even though there had been no upgrades to the gate, the wood didn't feel older or more rotted but rather at the same degradation as my memories. As we navigated the same gate process from fifteen years prior, with my mom pulling the car through, I remembered the secret hose. My memories of this place were in soft focus. Memories of memories. The last couple of years I'd thought of us racing from the spot my dad siphoned gas from the ground and I'd come to dispel it. There had been a couple shower sessions where I stood under running water, preoccupied, trying to think back on the hose and answer the question, "How exactly did my dad stop the gas from coming out? When it was all said and done?" I wouldn't ask this question of my parents or my sister, for fear they wouldn't know what I was talking about, or worse, tell me it was something I saw in a movie once. Was this another reason I wanted to come back to Maijoma after all this time? To figure out what was real. There was excitement in my throat as we went to close the gate. I prepared myself to look for any signs of our clandestine fuel stop.

As we finished closing the gate, my mom called out to my dad from the car.

"*¿Que es eso?*" my dad said as four uniformed men with large black guns approached us. The kind of guns one holds with two hands, like in the movies.

"Wait, is this another border check? But it's so far from the border? I don't remember this," I said to my parents as the men approached our car from all sides. One of the men started asking my parents questions in Spanish. They talked fast. Faster than my Iowa-Midwestern "took Spanish in high school" Spanglish could comprehend. The man's sentences were rapid fire but punchy. Short bursts of questions and commands. My parent's responses followed rhythm. I caught something about moving our car forward.

"*Mucho gusto y gracias,*" my dad said as he went to shake the initial man's hand. A USD bill transferred from one palm to the other mid-handshake. My dad and I joined my mom in the car. We pulled up and over a man lying on his back in a trench. Our car straddled the two sides of the hole in the ground as the man checked the undercarriage for whatever it was the uniformed men were looking for. We waited. Until finally one of them rapped on our trunk, signaled to us, "We're done here." The rest of the way to Maijoma was silence. The inside roof of our car replaced the scrolling landscape as I sprawled across the back seat. My dad's secret hose forgotten in blurred memories of passing mesquite and cacti.

II.

THE LAST HURDLE to get to Maijoma is a small stream in a valley running across the trail. Depending on the season, and how much the rain has affected the valley, it could mean getting your car stuck in mud and sediment. There was one time we had to wait before the rain cleared away, our parents stating that it would be too dangerous to attempt the crossing. Maria and I took turns skipping rocks on the water while we waited at the riverbank.

On this trip, the dirt at the bottom of the valley was dry and caked, as if the region hadn't seen rain since we last ran through it. We made quick work of the valley and turned onto the only trail that Maijoma called its own.

Along this trail, the first sign of a return to civilization was the school my dad went to as a child. Its courtyard doubled as the community center and makeshift volleyball court. Follow the trail past the school and you'd walk by a handful of adobe shacks. Then my grandparents' shack. There was a pigsty by the house and a tool shed that my father and *tíos* made themselves. Across a dirt road from my grandparents' shack was their neighbors', whose living room doubled as the town convenience store.

Right next to the store was a hill with the town's single white church at its peak. The church at the top of the hill was accessible by three sides, though rocks and cacti punctuated the paths. The north wall of the hill was a cliff, the walkway before the front door of the church had deteriorated and fallen away through time, leaving the only entrance to the church inaccessible. If you opened the door, it would swing over the valley below. I thought about children navigating the sharp edges and holds up the cliff, scattering rocks as they ascended the wall and pulled up to the front door.

The unkemptness of this church, its forbidden entrance, suggested apostasy. Of townsfolk decades past gazing upon vistas after mass. Our family would have fit right in. As a child I went to church with my parents every Sunday, though large parts of the all-Spanish mass lost me. I don't remember when we stopped going. There wasn't any one single event that caused it, but over time we became ex-Catholics. The last thing I remember about faith is getting yelled at in *el nombre de Jesús*.

The hill and its church loomed over my grandparents' house as we pulled up next to my *abuelo's trocka*. As we looked closer at the ancient truck, we saw our grandfather in the driver's seat, napping. Sunbeams accented his dark leather skin and shone through his straw cowboy hat. Our car doors slamming shut woke my abuelo from his slumber. His gaze revealed cloudy and cataract-wrought eyes. "Ah, *ya llegaste?*" my *abuelo* asked as he lumbered from his ancient pickup truck. It was the same truck Maria and I stole in our last visit.

"Sorry for waking you. A lot of things have changed," my dad said in Spanish as we gathered our things from the car.

"They always do. Like Angel here. You've grown!" my *abuelo* said as his eyes locked on mine. The bottom row of his teeth were a mash, specks of yellow bone and enamel. "Come in, your *abuela* is inside with Concha. She can help you bring in your things." My *abuelo* set the pace as we followed behind his ancient shuffle. A pack of baby ducks scurried along our feet as we opened the screen door to my grandparents' shack.

My *Tía* Concha, along with some other people I did not know, greeted us from inside. Everyone took turns shaking everyone else's hand, a strict custom that, growing up, my mom would be sure my sister and I would adhere to under her breath. *"Saludan a todos . . . a* everyone, Angel!"

As the salutations crossed onto one another, my attention turned to Concha, who was walking toward a bed in a room next to the kitchen. My *tía* picked up a spoon and began to feed a woman lying on the bed. The woman was old, older than *mi abuelo*, an invalid looking up at the ceiling, crumbling onto herself. Her skin creases on creases. An electric shock of emotion ran through me as I recognized the woman as my grandmother. What remained of *mi abuela*. Concha recognized my reaction as she wiped some food from my grandmother's chin.

"Yeah, it's been too long since you've seen your *abuela*, Angel. *Abuelita*. It's Angel." My grandma looked over at me in slow motion. Looked past me.

"Mucho gusto," she said, introducing herself. She strained to lift her hand in greeting.

Comparisons of the grandma I knew flooded my memory. During our last visit, Maria came up with the name "Ghetto Granny." Maria and I would walk around my grandparents' shack, bemoaning the lost comforts of our modern Midwestern home. "No Nintendo to play games on, no VCR to watch movies, not even a TV itself!" It was in this state that we came across my grandma, sweeping the dust from the house.

"Check out Ghetto Granny, she tough as shit walking around doing all this work," Maria whispered in my ear as we passed by. Both my grandparents were stoic people, but my grandma had what looked like a permanent scowl on her face as she worked on the

57

household chores.

"*Cuidado* . . . you kids don't know nothing!" she would yell at us in Spanish. She would warn us about staying away from cacti. Tell tall tales to scare us away from misbehaving. Invoke Christ to protect us from ourselves.

"Man, I'ma go find out what there is to do around here," Maria said to herself. I ran behind, catching the screen door before it slammed shut. Outside, we found out that compared to West Liberty, with its swimming pool, movie theater, parks, and friends, Maijoma was a lonely place for two siblings. We walked the dirt road to the end of the village and back. Walked the trails to the boarded-up church. Found what entertainment two kids from the Midwest could muster in a *pueblo* lost to time.

"Man, I wish there were some other kids here. Kids that we could play with," I said as I trailed behind my sister.

"You're always trying to play games and do kid stuff, Angel. It gets old fast," she replied over her shoulder.

"I mean, what are we supposed to do here? Mom and Dad are having all the fun with Dad's family. We're only here 'cause we can't stay at Iowa by ourselves."

"And what would you do if we were still in Iowa without Mom and Dad, Angel? Go ride bikes with your friends? Play hide and seek?"

"I mean. That sounds like fun, no?" I said while I tripped on some rocks. Maria stopped replying as she continued walking ahead of me. "What's your problem? You've been quiet and weird this trip. Since the *baile* in Ojinaga."

"It wasn't a fucking *baile*, Angel, it was a *quinceañera*," Maria said.

"What's the difference?" I asked.

"Nothing. Let's go back and mess with Ghetto Granny," Maria said as she kicked away a rock on the trail. As we came upon our grandparents' shack, our grandpa met us before the door.

"*Espersen. Mirar,*" my grandpa said to us. He extended his work-weary hand to give me a gift. Maria looked on as he presented me a handcrafted toy. He had gathered and carved sticks to make a gymnast, held between two poles. If you squeezed the bottom of the poles, the gymnast would somersault up and return to the bottom. And if you squeezed them just right, he could do a handstand at the top, suspended between two points.

"Thank y—*gracias!*" I said as I immediately started to manipulate the toy. Maria walked past us, through the beaten-up screen door.

That night the adults lit the oil lamps that looked like flowers. Started having conversations over dinner. I walked into the guest room Maria was staying in. She was facing an oil lamp on a pink nightstand on the opposite side of the bed, hunched over. Maria startled as I rounded the bed to find one of her legs crossed, pant leg up to expose her ankle. She had a sewing needle in her hand.

"Whoa," I said. "What are you doing?"

"Shhh," Maria whispered as she looked to make sure no one followed me. I looked at her ankle to see foreign symbols, numbers, and designs. Extravagant. Beside the oil lamp was a small container of ink. "For real, Angel, you can't tell anyone about this." My smirk exposed the thoughts of small blackmails I could lien against Maria in the future. Some of my *tíos* and male cousins had tattoos, inconspicuous things in easy-to-cover places. But it was a sin for any of the women in our family to get tattoos, let alone a tattoo so pronounced as the one Maria was working on. "Angel! For real, I'm fucking serious. You can't tell anyone. Promise?" She put aside the needle and extended her pinky.

"Okay, okay. I won't tell anyone." I said as I reciprocated my pinky in promise. Maria grabbed the needle between her thumb and index finger with intention. She dipped the needle in the vial of ink and brought it to her ankle. She punctured her skin with methodical rhythm. You could see the skin rise with each prick as it left the ink on its ascent. Dot by dot, prick by prick, she was shading in a big X, which was part of a bigger design I couldn't see past her cuffed jean leg. The tattoo danced in the oil lamp's flame.

"How long have you been doing this?" I asked.

She replied with a question of her own. "When you go out in West Lib with your friends, riding bikes and spending the night at their houses, you don't have to tell our parents where you go, right?" She surveyed her progress, never wincing or revealing if there was any pain. I thought about her question, about the last time I spent the night at Josh's and only told my mom about it the day after. "Well, I don't get to do that. If I'm out past six they have to know everything. And. They tell me I gotta be back by nine, no matter where I am. So . . ." She gestured to her leg. "I get lots of time to work."

A shriek in the kitchen interrupted Maria right as she was in the middle of a needle puncture. The noise caused her hand to slip and puncture her leg way past the point of the needle. She yanked the needle out and covered her mouth, stifling a yell of her own. In the commotion I knocked over the ink on the nightstand, the black splashed against pink. An instant Rorschach. We bumbled in the dim light, composed ourselves, and went toward the source of the shriek.

We found my grandma running around her bedroom, faster than any old person I've seen move. Her yelling was a result of putting on a slipper and feeling an *alacran* wiggle among her toes. As my sister and I came upon my grandma, she had a rolled-up paper in her hand, on the hunt for the scorpion. My sister was about to calm our *abuela* when she slammed the paper down on the scorpion. Maria jumped back from the sound as the rest of our family ran in, calming the situation down. Calming our grandma in hysterics. I looked at Maria and onto her now rolled-down jean leg. A spot of blood and ink was running through the denim of her Levi's.

∽

I remembered the effort my family had to make to calm my grandmother down. The speed and calamity that she evoked in killing the scorpion before us. It was difficult to reconcile that force with the husk of a woman that lay before me, who did not remember me. Vicks VapoRub, lit candles of unfamiliar saints, and the sour smell of my *abuela* herself filled my nostrils as I got close enough for *un saludar.* Her fragile bones waited in mine before she lowered her hand, turned her head, and fell asleep.

I retreated to the room where I had discovered Maria tattooing herself. I rubbed a splotch on the nightstand, trying to gauge whether it was the same ink that I knocked over. Maria never told me that the key ingredient to homemade tattoos was India ink. In junior high, a lot of us kids would try to emulate the tattoos our older siblings gave themselves. We would blow the ink out of ballpoint pens, but tattoos with regular ink deteriorated over time. Which we're thankful for now as the design and general look of our "scratchers" were atrocious. It must have been how methodical Maria was with her tattoos, but her work could pass for professional grade. Ours looked like chicken scratches, like the work of kids with unsure hands. It got so bad that the school admins got our classes together to warn us about the stupidity of our newfound hobby. They told us, "Wait until you're old enough to get professional work done." Which was good advice, but it's hard to curb kids trying to follow in their older siblings' footsteps.

The splotch on the nightstand rubbed off with ease. It wasn't the India ink, only accumulated grime or dirt. I walked out of the room and through the kitchen toward the outside screen door for some air. Before I reached it, my mom hollered at me from the table.

"Angel, can you go next door *a comprar botellas de soda por nosotros? La Coca* and *Esprite* for us tonight?" she asked.

"For real?"

"Como no? No te vayas caer again, right? You no gonna fall," she said with a smirk.

The screen door slammed shut as I heard my family already begin their side of the story. The story on the series of incidents between my sister and I that led to us almost killing each other. And how it all started with a pack of baby ducks and a case of Coca-Cola.

III.

IT WAS THE NIGHT after the scorpion incident during our childhood trip. After I discovered the hints of my sister's secret life etched on her leg. The adults were celebrating for no reason. I peeked around the kitchen to watch my grandma. She had cracked open a beer and was laughing with my parents, telling them a story. My eyes grew as I noted the way she would stop her story with a drink. She would raise her finger to let people know she would get back to it, taking deep sips of her beer with her eyes closed. My grandma caught me watching after I got too comfortable and leaned around the corner far enough for her to see me. She shifted her expression and placed her beer away from view.

After composing herself, she ordered me and my sister to to go next door and get some cases of pop for the festivities. It was a common thing for the elders to ask such an errand of the children at parties, usually because all the adults had been drinking and couldn't drive. In West Liberty this meant getting on our bikes and traveling across town for the errand. This wasn't the case in Maijoma, since the convenience store was in the living room of my grandparents' next-door neighbors' house.

My sister was already across the dirt path, among the rocks and cacti, up to the neighbor's door.

"Hey, wait up for me!" I yelled out as I navigated the terrain after her.

Now is a good time to describe my sister's and my physical stature fifteen years ago. Until recently, we were both small and skinny kids. But in the last year Maria had hit her growth spurt. She was taller but looked even skinnier, her limbs at the awkward, spindly stage of puberty. Despite still having to acclimate to her growing legs, Maria could hold her own on the junior high volleyball team. She wore knee-high socks to conceal her ink. My nine-year-old body was on the other side of puberty. I was a tiny kid with a big head, who would rather play on my Gameboy than join West Liberty's flag football leagues. These growing, spindly kids were the ones who stepped from rock to rock to make it up to the convenience store.

I joined my sister inside the store and used the opportunity. "So how long have you had the tattoos? Did they hurt? Like for real for real? Are you in a gang?"

"Angel. Shut. Up," Maria replied among the Mexican candy and snacks. "You promised not to tell."

The dark face at the counter kept his attention on a portable radio playing *Norteño bandas*.

"Like this guy can even understand us or knows who we are," I said while picking out favorites among the *Pelon Pelo Ricos, paletas, chicharrones de harina,* and other treats we recognized as the same ones in our Mexican *tienda* back home. "Okay, okay. One question. How do you get it past Mom when you have to wear dresses?"

"When's the last time you saw me wearing a dress?" Maria asked as we hit the back of the store and bottles of soda. It was a good point. Both my sister and I had moved away from the style of clothes our parents had bought for us as kids. If you were to look through our childhood photo albums, I would be in cowboy boots and hats. Like the clothes kids in Ojinaga wore as they wrestled at the *bailes.* Maria was clad in all manner of ornate dresses and fabrics, a little doll. As we figured out ourselves among the other '90s Iowan kids, we ditched the Mexican wear for tennis shoes and rad neon clothes. Only now, Maria started getting into flannels and Dickies, like in the movie *Mi Vida Loca* that she would always watch, about *cholas* in Echo Park. She would finish the VHS, immediately load it into our race-car tape rewinder, get to the beginning, and watch it again.

"So you're not going to wear dresses no more?"

"I don't know. We'll see," she replied as she bent over to carry two cases of soda on each other. She strained to get them over to the counter. We handed the man our parents' money, coins we had never seen before. They made sure the pesos were the right amount before we left the party. Maria attempted to pick up both cases for the trek home.

"Here, I can get the bottles of Coke," I said as I hoisted the top crate. The bottles were so tall they blocked my view.

"Yeah, right. You can't even see above them. Let me take them, kid," Maria said, emphasizing *kid.* I propped the door open with my foot, then turned and backed out of the store, case in hand, without saying a word.

Outside the store, we began the precarious journey back with our cases of bottles. It was halfway through the rocky terrain and into the dirt road when Maria saw the flock of ducks. A chain of yellow clumps, stumbling over themselves. Maria stopped, perplexed by the trills and chirps emanating from their tiny reed beaks. We looked on as the baby ducks climbed up the trail, toward the church on the hill. "Where are they going?" my sister asked herself as she

63

turned and began to follow.

There was a beat as I looked toward our grandparents' shack and then back at Maria, who was now in line with the ducks. They were picking up their pace, in a hurry, like they were late to church.

"Hey, wait up—" I tried to say as I turned and followed the group. But as I pivoted, my feet tripped on themselves and I fell. Face first. Onto my case of Coca-Cola bottles. The glass and soda exploded as the rest of my body collided with the rocks that were at my feet.

"Oh, shit!" my sister said as she dropped her case of bottles and ran to me. The immediate aftermath of my fall was a daze. There was glass all around me. The liquid in the bottles mixed with the dirt and created a sticky paste of glass and muck. I managed to get a view of the ducks as they hurried toward the church, startled by the sound of sixteen bottles of Coke all breaking in unison. My sister must've yanked me up and carried me to our grandparents' house. She bypassed the adults hanging out in the kitchen through a side door to her guest room. Next thing I know I was at the foot of her bed.

"Angel. Angel! Please, please. Don't cry. You're okay. I can fix this," my sister pleaded with me.

"What? What are you talking about, why should I cry?" I asked in a daze. And in that exact moment, when those two questions came out of me as I looked at my sister, the blood from the gashes burst forth as if on cue. Like the soda that had exploded from the bottles outside, the blood poured out from my cuts. From a nasty gash on my right eyebrow. I cried like I had never cried before.

"Ama!" I said at the top of my lungs.

"Shit, Angel, no!" My sister put her hands over my mouth but it was too late. This wasn't a stifled yelp but a full-on scream. My parents and *abuela*, moving with the same quickness that she had done the night before, were with us in the guest room. They stumbled on the shock of my sister with her hands over my mouth, stifling my hysterics as we both were now covered with dirt, dried soda, and blood. *Mi abuela* appeared next to Maria as my parents tended to my wounds. Later they would recall pulling shards of glass from their nine-year-old son's face.

64

Maria looked up to find Ghetto Granny over her.

"*Qué hiciste cabrona!*" *mi abuela* said to Maria as she grabbed her chin.

"Nothing! It wasn't my fault, he wanted to carry them too!" my sister said as she struggled to free her face. My grandma was unrelented in her grasp. In the panic of the room, my sister forgot that my grandma couldn't understand English. She might as well had been speaking in an alien language.

"Get off me!" Maria said with extra oomph as her struggles turned to a shove. My *abuela* stumbled back in surprise. Even I took pause from my bawling, realizing how big of an affront it was for a kid to touch a parent. After her surprise, my grandma scanned the room in silence, with contempt. My mom, still preoccupied with my wounds, yelled out to my sister to apologize to our grandma. Maria ignored her requests and pushed her way out the side door of the shack, to Maijoma's moonlit night.

∽

It was late. The errand to get a case of Coke in my adult years was less eventful. Like the soldiers that accepted my dad's bribe, the neighbors accepted my U.S. dollars as payment. We were close enough to the border that both pesos and U.S. currency circulated freely. When I entered the store, I realized two things: that the place was tiny, and that they no longer even sold bottles. They had the same cans of pop we had in Iowa.

In the guest bathroom, the dull light bulb over the mirror flickered as I looked at myself. About ten years after my run-in with the case of Coca-Cola bottles, the government surveyed the 160 townsfolk of Maijoma. The 80 men and 80 women deliberated whether they wanted a cellphone tower or electricity for the town. They chose the more foundational of the two options.

I thought about their decision as I pulled out my phone, a glorified brick in my hand here. I noted that there wasn't anything even resembling cell reception out here. My thumb flicked the phone open as I scrolled through my contacts. The scrolling names landed on "Maria." Quick, to not take it back, I deleted the contact and flicked the phone shut. My eyes took a moment to adjust past the grime in the mirror as I stared at my reflection. My hand lifted, over to the scar on my eyebrow.

Immediately after my sister walked out of the room the night of the Coke incident, my grandpa got out some tools and an apple. He pantomimed for me to turn my head and take a bite at his go. As I bit into the apple, he used a needle and thread to sew up the gash on my eyebrow. Halfway through the procedure, I dropped the apple and panicked.

My grandma snapped at me as she recovered the fruit. *"Cálmate,* Angel!" I calmed down at the threat of added punishment from Ghetto Granny.

Looking over his work in the bathroom mirror, I have to say that *mi abuelo* did a good enough job. Most people don't notice the scar until I point it out.

∽

A couple of days passed before my sister and I started talking again. The oppressive boredom prevailed over our reluctance to hash out the aftermath of my fall. Staying in Maijoma was like being on a permanent Sunday afternoon. Those Sundays where the excitement and fun of a sleepover were behind you. Your friends were back at their own homes. There was nothing on TV to watch. The looming ennui of a Monday school day clung to your every action. Fighting or not, my sister and I didn't stand a chance against perpetual Sunday by ourselves. Well, that and the questions we both had as we crossed each other on the paths leading up to the church on the hill. Where were those baby ducks going, and where were they now?

Maria gestured to my stitches. "Did it hurt?" I didn't regale her with the story of dropping the apple and bawling like a baby until Grandma calmed me down.

"Nah not too bad . . . but are you mad at me or something?" I asked as we synced our strides up the trail.

"Yeah, I'm mad, Angel. You didn't do shit when that lady got at me. It wasn't my fault. I never asked you to follow me," Maria said as we made short work of the trail and reached the dilapidated church, scanning the ground and listening for peeps. We set off to descend from the opposite trail down the other side of the hill.

"I was kinda distracted," I said to myself as I pulled out the wooden toy my grandpa made for me. It was still a challenge to get the guy to balance just right at the top.

"Well, it's a good thing she didn't try to do anything but grab me. I won the last fight I got into," Maria said as she scooted around a cactus.

The gymnast fell limp between my fingers. "You've gotten into a fight?" I asked.

Maria ignored my question. We made quick work of the other trail and were now at the bottom of the hill, facing the cliff wall that composed the hill's north side. The wall loomed over us as I strained to make out the church door overlooking the town. It was about five times our height. It reminded me of the cover of *Banner in the Sky*, a book Maria read for class, with a boy scaling a cliff among other mountaintops on the horizon. Maria surveyed the wall and looked over at me.

"Yeah, I've gotten into some fights. You wouldn't know 'cause you're too busy playing. Come on. Bet you they're inside," she said as she started to climb.

"Wait, what? We can't climb that!" I said as I put the gymnast in my back pocket.

"Why not? What else is there to do?" Maria yelled out to me, already a quarter of the way up the wall.

"I can't," I said, defeated. By that time in my life, my fear of heights was palpable. I'd close my eyes and my palms would get sweaty every time my dad drove across a tall bridge.

"Fine then. Don't expect me to tell you what I find when I bust in that church!" Maria yelled out. She was making quick work of the wall. Her sinewy arms moved fast and fluid. Her speed surprised me, caught me off guard. Before I knew it, she had reached the final stretch, and I realized that attempting the climb to catch up to her was a lost cause.

"Wait!" I yelled as I ran up a side trail, careful not to trip on any rocks along the way. If I didn't have the guts to climb the wall and see inside for myself, at least I could see Maria enter the church from the side.

As I caught my breath at the side of the church, I craned my neck around the wall to scan the entrance and cliff below. No Maria. Nothing. I hollered my sister's name, hoping that she would reply from inside the church. Maybe she found a secret side entrance she could let me in from? No answer. I hollered a few more times before realizing that even if Maria could hear me, she wouldn't answer back. She was gone. I walked back down the side of the hill to our grandparents' house, ashamed I wasn't brave enough to scale the wall with Maria proper.

My grandma interrupted my malaise as she snapped at me from outside the house. "Is your sister in our church?" she asked in Spanish.

I stammered out a "N-No. We were playing, that's it!" My grandma ignored my answer.

"In the church? You better not have been in there. That's a sacred place. No place for children who . . ." she trailed off, then said to herself, "I'll wait for her."

Maria, running toward the house from afar, interrupted my schemes to distract my *abuela*. She was hollering my name before she saw her waiting beside me. Maria dragged to a walk and stopped before us, dusting off her jeans.

"You were in the church," my grandma said. It was not a question. Maria looked at me with accusatory eyes. I protested back to her in silence that Granny had ambushed me too.

"No, I wasn't," Maria replied. "I was walking around, checking it out."

"That's not what Angel said," my grandma replied. "Admit it." A chill ran up my spine. Maria's accusatory stare dissipated, the fire and anger extinguished. She thought I had betrayed her. I should have protested. I should have yelled out that my grandma was lying. Instead, I put my hands in my pockets and looked away.

"I didn't go in. I tried, okay? But I couldn't get in," Maria said.

That was enough for my *abuela*. "What use is that church if you kids don't even believe in God?" she said. Spanish words spat out like acid as she rushed back to her house to talk with her son about us, navigating the dust and rocks with ease.

When she was outside of earshot, I immediately started pleading with Maria. "I didn't say any—"

"Stop! It don't even matter. You gotta check this shit out," Maria said with youthful fervor. She was already running back the trail she came from. She got in the church. She must have. Flashes of treasure and mystery flooded my mind as I ran to catch up. When we got to the base of the cliff, I could see the church door was open.

"So, I can tell you what's in there. Or you can see for yourself. What do you wanna do?" Maria asked.

Pangs of fear reverberated through my arms. In my gut. My sister was never one to let you off the easy way. I knew that if I let her simply tell me what was inside, something would be lost between us. I grabbed ahold of the wall above me and hoisted myself up. From my perch, I looked over, face to face with Maria.

"I can do this."

"Okay. Let's go. I'm behind you," she said as she followed suit.

About halfway up the cliff, I realized I wasn't as good of a climber as my sister. Besides some key trees in town, there weren't many good climbing spots in West Liberty. Sometimes we would try to climb up the side of The Tornado, a spiraling slide in Kimberly Park that was not too far from our house. But we were already past the height of that slide and still had a ways to go. It was about twice as long as Maria's climb, but we were inching our way up.

"Keep going, Angel. I'll break your fall. If you fall, I fall," Maria kept saying to me, like a mantra. The spoils of a forbidden church motivated me more than the idea of us falling together. My forearms ached as Maria coached me on the last couple of holds to get to the top.

"Almost there," Maria said to me. Right before she reached up her hand for a hold, a tarantula scurried from the rocks she brushed away. *La araña.* She let out a yelp. The sound of her surprise is forever associated with the image I saw as I pulled myself over the top of

69

the cliff. My eyes adjusted to the church door wide open before me. Here is what I saw in that split second, burned in my memory.

It is a jungle. Verdant. Foliage bursting from the walls. Big caricatures of leaves. Imagine taking a jungle and stuffing it into a tiny room. There are wood chairs overcome by vines. A thick carpet of moss adorns the back wall like a fresh patch of sod uprooted from the ground and grown on its side. Poking out among the moss and foliage is a skewed crucifix of Jesus. The cross is so sideways that it looks like the nail in Jesus' wrist holds up his figure. He wears vegetation like a blanket. And there they are, the baby ducks, bathing in a pool on the ground. Shaking and chirping with life. This is it, the promised treasure.

Words escaped me as I looked down at Maria, who no longer was right below me but rather lying lifeless at the base of the hill.

"Maria!" I cried out as I half climbed half slid half fell down the cliff. The rocks and edges scratched me, tore into my clothes. Cuts and bruises covered my body as I reached my sister. "Maria!" I said again as I shook her awake. She cried out in protest, wincing from the pain.

"Careful, careful," she said as she sat up. "Shit, that hurt."

"What happened?" I asked.

Maria told me about the spider. How she lost her hold and tumbled down the wall, tried to regain her grip and smacked her head along the way. The area around her right eye was pink. It would turn into a black eye by the end of the week. I helped Maria to her feet as we surveyed the damage.

"Did you see it?" Maria whispered.

Before I could answer, our grandma was on us. She had gathered the rest of our family. She wanted to catch us in the act of breaking in to the church, to expose our nefarious schemes to our parents. Instead, they came across two beat-up and bloody kids far away from home. My parents immediately pushed past my grandma and went into damage control mode. They asked if my stitches were still in, took turns looking at my sister's eye.

Amid the commotion, I noticed some sticks by Maria's foot. It was the toy my grandpa made. Mangled and broken. My stomach lurched as I realized what the pile actually was. I hunched over to pick up the remains, and saw that Maria's jeans had ripped during her fall, from the cuff to her knee. A snag on some foliage among the rocks. Her secret tattoos laid bare.

I tried to warn her while stuffing the broken toy in my pocket, but it was too late.

"*¿Qué es esto?*" my grandma asked with alarm. She staggered back from the sight of Maria's leg. All eyes on that bare leg. My parents joined in my *abuela's* shock.

Now, here's the thing. By that time in our short lives, our parents spared my sister and me from any real corporal punishment. My cousin Freddy would extol the virtues of packing your wallet with baseball cards to buffer any spankings from my *tía*, but our parents didn't get at us too bad. It's become something of a joke, the concept of Mexican grannies and *la chancla,* but when you're a kid and you really mess up, the last thing you want to see is a pissed-off grandmother. Maria's exposed tattoo was a mess-up beyond anything us kids could imagine. Maria braced herself as my *abuela* moved on her.

It must have been the adrenaline, from climbing the cliff, seeing an oasis, or thinking my sister was dead, but I blocked Maria from impending doom. My arms stretched wide as I shielded my sister from the beating she was sure to get. My grandma shoved me away as she got a better look at the sacrilege etched on her granddaughter's leg. I shut my eyes for the ensuing smack that would be echoing from the cliff walls.

Only it didn't. What emanated from our grandma was much worse. When the sounds of violence never came, I opened my eyes to find my grandma in tears. Slow at first. Then her tears turned into a wail I had never heard before. *La Llorona.* Deep, resonant sobs from her belly.

"*No. ¿Por qué? ¡Pobrecita, por qué!* What did you do, *chamaca?*" she said between her cries. "*¡Aye Dios, no sabe que hizo!*"

Our *abuelo* comforted the convulsing woman. I looked at Maria for a sign on what to do, how to react to this outpouring. We had made adults mad before, furious even, but we had never broken anyone. Maria returned my glance. She had tears in her eyes. The tears of a kid who realized she crossed a point she could never come back from.

71

Maria steeled herself, wiped her tears away. "Fuck this," she said, and ran back to my grandparents' house. My family let her pass as they went to calm the woman in hysterics. I thought about going to abuela too but remembered it, our secret jungle. I ran after my sister.

Before I could get to the shack, I found Maria in our grandpa's *trocka*. She was waiting for me.

"What are you doing?" I asked, thinking she was in enough trouble.

"Let's go. Let's get the hell out of this place. Only for a bit," she said, looking forward to the road ahead. Her dried tears had made streaks down the dirt on her face.

"Let's go then," I said. And I got into the passenger seat.

IV.

EL SOL HUNG HIGH as I walked away from the church that loomed over my family fifteen years ago. The church whose door was agape as a kid got the teensiest peek at bliss. My shoulder ached as I navigated the rocks down the trail. There was no death-defying climb this time, no falls either. It was almost funny how simple it was this time. I walked up to the side of the church and reached my foot far enough to make it to the isolated front entrance. This point of entry out of reach to our pubescent limbs way back when. Then it was a matter of a firm-enough shoulder to break open the door.

There was nothing. A small room full of cobwebs and rocks. Not a speck of vegetation. I stood in the room silent, filled with doubts and questions. Could the village have moved everything out since the last trip? Was it a mirage, a child's imagination run wild with boredom? Or had we tainted it, this sacred place? I dragged the door shut behind me, vowing never to return.

These questions still stirred in my head as I stumbled into *mi abuela's* room. "Oh! *Lo siento,"* I said, surprised to find my *Tía* Concha in the room. My tía had my *abuela* sitting up as she rinsed her back with a wet rag. I averted my eyes as I realized the gown my grandma usually worn was undone and around her stomach. Her bare breasts

72

and stomach were a tapestry of scars, sores, and wrinkles. A life's worth of accumulated wear. My face grew hot and I turned to walk out the door when my grandmother recognized me.

"*¿Concha? ¿Es Angel?*" she asked as my *tía* helped get her gown back over her shoulders.

"*Sí Ama, es Angel. Está aquí con tu hijo,*" my aunt replied.

"*¿Y Maria? ¿Dónde está tu hermana?*" my grandma asked with pointedness.

My *Tía* Concha's eyes grew wide as she looked at me from behind my grandma. I looked at my *abuela*, at this woman who had been such a defining force in my memory. This larger-than-life person filled with passion, anger, and lamentations over us. Who could never understand us but left an imprint on us all the same. I thought about her misunderstandings, her expectations of us. I thought about my sister.

"She left us," I said in English before I walked out the door to *mi abuelo's* ancient truck. The keys were in the ignition. The same as when my sister came across them fifteen years ago.

∽

It took Maria more than a couple of minutes to get the hang of the truck's stick shift, to stop mangling the gears as we made it to the end of the village trail. Once we got to the end of the trail, we kept on going, away from the village on rougher and rougher terrain.

"Are you okay?" I asked.

Maria kept her eyes on the trail ahead. "Yeah I'm fine, got the wind knocked out of me *pos muy gacho*. But beside that and my eye, I'm fine."

"You look like shit," I replied. Maria laughed. A big yawping laugh like everyone in my family does when they find something for real for real funny.

"We both do, little brother. We both look beat up all to shit," she said after she finished laughing. "But nah, that's not what really hurt though, ya know?"

73

"Yeah, I know. So, you okay?" I asked again.

"I will be. Are you?" she replied.

I grasped at my wooden toy, mangled and heaped in my pocket. In that moment I realized I wouldn't be able to fix the figure my grandpa made for me. I clenched my teeth and squeezed the debris in my fist. The wood cracked and splintered as it dug into my palm. I still remember how it felt in my hand. Losing something as a child transcends time.

"I will be. We both will."

We were well outside any trails close to Maijoma, having driven an hour away from the village. In that time, we did something we had never done before. We talked. As equals. We talked about what her tattoos meant. We talked about how she broke into the church. I think we talked about the gardens growing inside, but I doubt myself now. We talked about our fears.

"So what are you scared of, Angel?"

"When I was little, Grandma would say I was going to hell. That scared me. Remember that? When she would say we'd go to hell for playing around at the dinner table."

"Yeah, I remember. We would always be messing around though. Annoying her and being loud," Maria said with a chuckle.

"It used to keep me up at night," I replied as I looked out the passenger-side window, at more and more cacti. The flora seemed to engulf us.

"You not scared of hell no more?" Maria asked.

"I'm more scared that there's nothing. No hell. No heaven. That there's nothing but us and when it's over, it's over," I replied.

"Yeah. I'm scared that Grandma's wrong too," Maria said.

It wasn't much longer before two things dawned on us: a gate blocking our path and the realization that we might not be able to find our way back. Maria churned the truck to a stop.

"What do we do?" I asked.

"We made it this far. We just got to cross," she replied with a voice I wasn't prepared for. The voice of someone unsure, looking for something.

The adrenaline of our day was long gone. Exhaustion was setting in. The ramifications of what we had done, what we were still doing, were beginning to weigh on us. Something told me that my grandma's pity would revert to swift justice at our prolonged joy ride. We were going farther from anything that we knew, that we could go back to.

"I'm scared," I said as I looked at my sister.

"Please, Angel," she said. Her voice a crack. A whisper in her throat.

We opened the gate and pulled through. We drove one last stretch of landing before a river finally cut off our dirt path. My sister and I marveled at the scene before us. Across from the river there was a hut, but not like my *abuelo's* homemade cement and stucco house. This looked different, less permanent. The same vegetation from inside the church had sprouted from the riverbanks and worked its way to surround the hut. Maria shut off the truck and we walked out to get a closer look. Beside the hut, there was a single clothesline, hung up between pomegranate trees. The sound of running water intermingled with the sounds of birds we could not see, hiding in the trees engulfing the house.

We had been standing by the riverbank for what seemed like an hour when the front door opened. A woman walked out with a rusted tin of clothes to dry. She wore a thin frock dyed a dull red, without any of the embroidery that adorned my grandma's dresses. Her hair, dark like ours, was in a long braid down her back. Her skin was a reddish bronze, like clay, like our skin when went to the pool everyday in the summer. Maria and I had driven far enough from our family that we stumbled on someone living completely off the land. The woman didn't notice us as she began to hang her clothes on the line. We watched in silence as she worked.

"Where are we?" I whispered to Maria "Is this lady all by herself out here?"

It took a long time for Maria to reply. I watched her watch the woman working in the breeze. Maria turned away from the fantasy laid before us and took my hand. "Come on. We bothered her enough. Let's go home."

∽

I'm not ashamed to admit that my sister had a better handle of our grandpa's truck fifteen years ago than I managed in the present day. The ancient transmission sputtered at my hands. I tried my best to trace the route we had made away from Maijoma.

It wasn't long before my surroundings were completely foreign to me, before I became lost on foreign trails. You can't fathom the terror of getting lost until you are in the middle of a desert with no familiar landmarks in any direction. When the very real possibility of abandonment creeps up, of no one finding you for days, or weeks. What was I doing here? On these paths and on this trip?

My hands gripped the wheel tight as the frustration over the last few days raced through my mind. Frustration at the dashing of my memories by reality, by an adult's eye. Frustration at myself for not fully answering my grandmother's question on where my sister was. Saying that Maria left us was too simple. The brevity of my answer wasn't another example of the language barrier between us. Even if I spoke Spanish fluently, I would not have been able to tell my grandma the full story.

Maria had chosen to stay in West Liberty instead of visiting Maijoma. To take care of her daughter. She had many valid reasons to stay home, the main one being she had drifted away from our family the last few years, as all kids do when they begin to raise their own kids. Maybe she knew what would happen if she came back, that it would confirm what she already knew about the stories we told each other. That a recollection of this place from our childhood would mutate and grow. That our imaginations as Midwestern kids would conflate the dreams of Maijoma with the reality of a village wracked with poverty and the passage of time. Is the magic of childhood tricks of perspective that adulthood pulls into focus?

I sped up the truck, but there was no outrunning yourself out here. Fear set in as I realized I was still scared of the nothingness I told Maria about on our truck ride. Only this time being alone compounded the dread of nothingness around me. It wasn't that she left us, or that she left me; it was that we got older and left each other.

And like that, the gate from our childhood appeared before me. I stalled the truck, shocked that I managed to retrace our path through my distress. A fresh aluminum sign shone at the gate. My stomach dropped as I noticed the contrast between fresh metal and dilapidated wood and wire.

"What? No . . . no no no," I said to myself in a daze, my voice foreign to me. A tiny voice from the back of my throat. The sign warned of shooting trespassers, and the mechanism to open the gate was on the other side. I thought of the men from the checkpoint before we got to Maijoma. Of politics and sovereignties expanding and contracting. I thought of acts of recklessness by my sister and me. Carrying boxes of Coke that were taller than I was. Going back to climb a cliff wall. Stealing this truck. Choosing the path wrought with unsureness to find treasures untold. I walked along the gate until I found a section cut open along the ground. I crawled on my belly through the opening, caking my clothes in earth.

My palms were sweating as I opened the gate and realized the severity of this last act of recklessness. What would happen if uniformed men stopped me? If I tried to communicate with them with my mangled, cobbled-together Spanish? The adrenaline and fear pushed me forward. I needed to see it, this one last thing, if it was real. The truck churned forward after closing the gate behind me. The sun was beginning to set, the dusk reds and purples that burned the landscape. The kind of sunset you take a picture of with your phone and immediately delete because the record can never match the magnificence before you.

A year after our last visit to Maijoma, Maria had her *quinceañera*. It went without a hitch, besides me flubbing a couple of the ceremonial steps as a *chambelan*. Maria had a full billowing white-and-pink dress with a hoop skirt that fell all the way to the floor. A year after the ceremony to welcome her to adulthood, I found my sister sneaking out of her bedroom one last time. As she shuffled backward onto the roof, I could feel something was different.

"What's going on?" I said. "Is everything alright?"

"Yeah, Angel. It's gonna be alright, but I gotta get out of here. Don't follow me and don't tell Mom, okay? Promise?" she said to me with the same look she gave me before the last gate in the desert.

"You're leaving," I said.

"Don't follow me, Angel. Not this time."

"What should I do?" I asked.

"Please, Angel," she said. And she climbed off the roof with the same quickness and fluid movement that she climbed up the cliff of the church long ago.

She ran off to live the life she needed, out from under our family's roof. She met a guy and had a child. I remember being a freshman in high school while Maria gave a talk as a senior. She talked about her path to having a kid at sixteen. This all pissed off my parents, of course. But they realized the stubbornness of their children and tried to work things out with Maria, with the guy. He split after a couple of months and Maria raised her daughter alone.

We haven't talked since. Some small chitchat, sure, but not really talking, like we did in this truck. The distance between us widened as our paths continued to diverge, with her raising a family and me going to community college. We've tried at different times to reach out to each other. I cancelled plans with her, for reasons I can't remember. We bumped into each other in front of a Chinese takeout joint one time. We attempted to catch up before we both found ways to excuse ourselves. The last time we "talked" was during the holidays. Maria sat by me at the dinner table, our utensils scraping the plates as we ate, filling the silence.

"Shit," I said to myself as two spots of light shone in my rearview mirror. They were dots, miles away, but they were also car headlights coming along the same path I was. "No, no, no." I drove faster. This wasn't the right path. Nothing was familiar. I was miles away from the spot, if there ever was a spot. This was a stupid idea. The ramifications of our past misadventures flashed through my mind. Splitting my eyebrow open on a case of Coca-Cola. Falling down a cliff wall. Stealing this truck because I was trying to find something I lost a long time ago.

As I wiped the sweat from my palms, two things happened. The lights grew in my rearview mirror before turning off a different road, and I found our riverbank.

My *abuelo's* truck kicked up dirt as it ground to a stop before the flowing current. Across from me was the house. I let out a noise a little kid would make when playing on the playground, or snaking around dancing parents at a *baile*. A yawp and a squeal. A physical

78

reaction to the scene before me.

It was the house. The same one, only basking in the hues of a setting sun. The trees that surrounded the hut were bigger than I remembered. The clothesline was the same, only now, it was full of clothes swaying in the wind. It was real. It was before me.

I sat for a long time, studying the house. Finally I got out of the truck and took out my phone. I contemplated taking a picture before it got too dark, but the house looked so sad in the small screen before me. Before I flicked the phone closed, it chirped and vibrated in my hand. I startled at the realization that there was a sliver of a bar of service here.

"You got to be kidding me," I said as my phone vibrated with delayed texts and voicemails. Messages sent my way during the trip, cascading upon my phone all at once. Maria's phone number flashed across the screen for an instant, before giving way to other notifications. A text with no contact attached, just the number. But I recognized it without her name, I had it memorized. I could feel the warmth of the setting sun dissipate. Like a roaring fire reduced to embers. I rubbed my thumb over my phone and looked at the vision before me.

The red and purples of the dusk are giving way to night. The river reflects the sky, turning into ink, turning into oil. The screen door swings open from across the river.

A woman holding a laundry basket backs up through the door to hold it. A small child waddles through the doorway and leads the way toward the clothesline. My eyes follow the pair as the woman hands the child garments and the child places them in the basket. They work preemptively. It begins to rain. The child laughs and begins to play in the now-forming mud. Quick, to force myself to commit, I scroll to Maria's number and call. The line rings as I bring it up to my ear. I hold my head up to the sky and let the rain hit my face. The rain is cold. With big fat drops that sting as they hit.

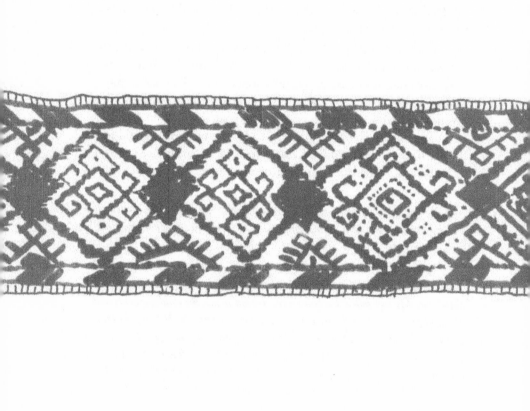

SADAGAT ALIYEVA

ARTIST STATEMENT

I grew up on the shore of the Caspian Sea in a small town, Turkan, on the Absheron Peninsula, near Baku, the capital of Azerbaijan. Baku is famous for its oil, but most people probably don't know that Baku is also known as the city of art and culture. The Absheron Peninsula is a small desert-like land known for its grapes, fig trees, and pomegranate trees. There were eight kids in my family, and each of us had one fig tree in our yard. I remember as a child how impatiently I waited for the first figs to ripen and to brag about seeing the first fruit before anyone else. I made friends with one of the pomegranate trees in the yard, and every night, when everyone had gone to bed, I would sneak out to talk with my tree, to tell her all my troubles. And I believed she always helped me by listening to me and tenderly shaking her branches.

As a child, fairy tales and myths fascinated me. My mom used to tell us stories before bed that I never found in any book. I learned to read early, and I devoured any book of tales I could find in the library. I grew up hearing ghazal, a form of poetry, and Mugam, a type of folk music, which deeply rooted in my soul. There are many many classical writers and poets who inspired me: Nizami, Mehseti, Fuzuli, Nesimi, Natavan, Shahriyar, Cavid . . . The Book of Dede Korkut is like a holy book. Its stories full of wisdom always inspired me.

I grew up at the crossroads of the Middle East/Asia and Europe: two different cultures, two different philosophies, two different visions. I grew up at the crossroads of ancient poetry, music, and folk art and Soviet realism. On one hand the beauty of patterns, textiles, color, and desert sands, and on the other hand, jazz, modern art, and European theater.

When I came to Iowa, the first thing that amazed me was the great kindness I experienced in people. Iowans welcomed my family and me. They gave us a home. I've met people here who helped me to find peace, freedom, and myself. Azerbaijan planted a storyteller in me, and Iowa watered and cared for this plant, helping it to grow and bloom. Azerbaijan is the land of miniature art, handwoven carpets, and stories that sank in my soul and shaped an ancient storyteller in me. Iowa is the land of diverse cultures, great opportunities, and fresh soil for new ideas and creativity that opened a path for that storyteller to reach out to a new world.

I'm telling the stories of my ancestors in a new language.

TWO LITTLE COTTAGES

Sadagat Aliyeva

IN A TINY TOWN there were two little cottages. A little girl lived in the Little Violet Cottage on top of the hill, and a little boy lived in the Little Green Cottage at the bottom of the hill. Although they never talked with one another, they often thought about each other.

"Wouldn't it be nice if he asked me to play with him sometime?" The thought passed through the girl's mind each time she noticed the boy biking up the hill. "I really like the way his curly hair flops on his forehead. I wonder if he likes me. I wonder if he has a lot of friends, if he even notices me around here."

The boy would think, "Her blue eyes sparkle like stars. I have never seen anyone with eyes like those before. I wonder if she sees I'm biking by her cottage. I wonder if she notices me, if she knows how badly I want to talk with her."

"Why doesn't he say hi to me, just once, just one little word, hi? It doesn't take much. We are neighbors, after all, and we both go to the same school. He passes by my cottage every day. If he doesn't like me, why does he climb up the hill to pass by? There are different roads around here. If he chooses to take this road, wouldn't it be nice to say hello?" Such thoughts made the girl mad. Then she thought, "Maybe I should talk with him." That made her nervous but sounded a good idea at the same time. Suddenly, another worrisome thought filled her head. "What if he makes fun of me and then tells jokes about me at school?" She became frightened and hid behind the curtains as if the boy were nearby.

The boy had fearful thoughts as well. First he thought, "I'll go talk with her tomorrow," and right away a scary question popped in his mind. "What if she says, 'Leave me alone' or 'Go away'? Why would she talk with someone like me, anyway? What is special about me? I bet she has a lot of friends and all of them admire her. Her long, wavy, golden hair, sparkling sky-blue eyes, those cute dimples that appear when she smiles . . ." The boy smiled too when he imagined her.

Days, months, and years passed. As they grew older, life became busier with new friends and new challenges. They thought of each other less and less each day but still did not dare to talk to one another or catch each other's eye when they passed by.

One day the boy packed his suitcase. He was going away, to the big city to start a new journey. The girl also was ready to leave the tiny town for a bigger adventure.

The train line was near her house, so the station was very close. She took an early afternoon train.

The boy missed his train in the morning. First, it made him upset, but then he said to himself, "I guess I'll take the next one." He hugged everyone goodbye one last time and left the house.

The girl was already on the train. Her eyes welled up with tears while she blew last kisses to her mom and dad standing on the platform and waving back at her, sending kisses. They were hiding their tears from her to not to add more to her nervousness. It's never easy to say goodbye. Her heart trembled a little: going to the big, strange city, with lots of people. What if she couldn't make friends? What if she ended up staying on the street like a tree and nobody even noticed her? How hard was it going to be, studying at the college? What if she didn't even like that city and ended up lonely, sad, and scared?

Walking toward the train, the boy turned his eyes to see for the last time the Little Violet Cottage that the girl lived in. He sighed and entered the train. While looking for a seat, his mind was wandering: "I don't even know where am I going or what's waiting for me. I don't know anyone there. How am I going to fit in?" Deep inside in his heart, there was a little fear bothering him.

He saw an open seat from afar, and as he walked closer, he found a young woman was sitting in the next seat. Noticing that someone was standing close to her, she raised her eyes. She was the girl from the Little Violet Cottage. The boy was astonished! Then he felt he had to speak, to say something to break the awkward silence.

"Hi," he said.

"Hi," said the girl and smiled. The boy smiled too.

"May I?" He pointed to the open seat.

"Please." The girl picked up her bag from the seat. The boy sat and looked at the girl. The girl smiled again.

"I'm Fea," she said.

"Sam," said the boy and shook the hand the girl extended. The two hands melted together. They raised their eyes and smiled at each other. Her blue eyes were sparkling like the stars. His golden curls were hanging down on his forehead.

They talked all the way to the city and never noticed that they were still holding hands.

The two little cottages in a tiny town stood smiling at their new journey and waited for the new stories to begin.

FOUR BROTHERS

Sadagat Aliyeva

ONCE UPON A TIME there were four brothers: Chatter, Toil, Battle, and Wisdom. Chatter was tall and skinny with long, tousled hair. Constant movement of his body and wild gestures caused his long curls to fling about his neck when he spoke. He was so loud that no one else could be heard. Narrowing his eyes, he talked quickly and nonstop, spraying his listeners with spittle.

Short in height but robust and hardy, Toil was always busily moving things around. He was so strong that he could pull a tall tree from the ground, complete with all its roots, using just one hand. When there was nothing more to do, Toil emptied out his already tidy and organized toolshed and organized it over and over again.

Tallest and strongest of all the brothers, Battle fought against everything, good or bad. From a distance you could notice him on horseback, riding rapidly from field to field, swinging his sword in the air.

Wisdom was small and thin, quiet and still. No one paid any attention to him. Slowly, the others forgot he even existed.

One day the three brothers Chatter, Battle, and Toil gathered together and shared an idea to go change the world in the way they knew the best. The three brothers walked through wide lands, beyond green forests and beautiful meadows.

They climbed over sandy hills and tall mountains, passed through distant towns, tiny villages, and nomadic tribes. They swam through mighty oceans, deep seas, and long rivers until they reached the edges of the Earth.

On their journey the brothers met people of all kinds, and wherever they went, they taught the people what they knew the best. Chatter taught them how to talk without listening. Toil demonstrated how they could move things around faster. Battle trained them how to fight against anyone and everything.

Consequently, the world became louder, busier, and angrier

87

every day. Before winter, people already were making summer plans. There was a fight against anything and everyone. Conversations became nothing but quarrels. And soon nobody knew what was actually right and what was wrong.

The days grew long and tiresome. Very soon the people of the world forgot friendship and how to be compassionate with one another. Joy and creativity slowly faded away from people's lives. The brothers became confused by the turmoil they created. It was clear they had made the world worse, not better. "But why," they wondered, and "What was our mistake?"

Very soon the people of the world tired of fighting all the time. Noise made them sad and exhausted. They became overwhelmed by so much action. Finally, they had to stop.

Silence slowly filled the air. Suddenly, they heard a whisper. Wisdom was talking to them; his voice was soft and comforting, his words soothing. He said, "Change happens from the inside."

"From the inside?" someone asked. "But how can we notice the change?"

"Close your eyes and look inward," Wisdom answered.

And they did. Multitudes of people all around the world settled down, closed their eyes, looked inward, and listened.

"Yes, I see," said the Elder, breaking the silence. "A lot has changed since the beginning."

"I don't see! Tell me!" the Child pleaded.

And the Elder began telling a story: Once upon a time . . .

FIRST THERE WAS LOVE

Sadagat Aliyeva

FIRST THERE WAS LOVE. And love was everything.

Waters washed the surface of the land, kissing each grain of sand. Sunrays gently caressed the little waves while spreading their warmth. Tree branches held nests tenderly, watching baby birds patiently, saving them from harm to grow and fly. Flying from flower to flower, butterflies spread love for creation. Moonbeams peeked through tiny windows on quiet nights to deliver magical dreams to little sleepy heads.

In this time, a baby girl was born into the soft and warm arms of Mother. Mother cuddled the child, sharing love with all her heart.

Girl awoke each morning to the sounds of birds singing on the branches near her window. As she grew, she ran with the wind, flew with the butterflies, sang with the birds, and jumped with the waves all day long. Mother brushed her hair tenderly, made her dresses as beautiful as colorful wildflowers, fed her with love, and told her story after story about ancient knights and faraway kingdoms, hags and clever princesses.

At night, when all lively beings were going to sleep, Girl lay in tender, motherly arms, closed her eyes, and melted away into a sweet lullaby:

> Laylay dedim yatasan *
> Qızıl gülə batasan
> Qızıl gülün içində
> Şirin yuxu tapasan
> Laylay gülüm a laylay
> Şirin dillim a laylay

Love spread its arms everywhere. Time passed as a sweet dream, and the child grew joyfully within the love of her mother. When the time came, Mother sent Girl to school. Walking her to the door to

90

say goodbye, Mother told Girl she would miss her and would wait impatiently for her return while making the most delicious food, her favorites, dolma, dovga, or pilov, for she would be hungry.

As soon as Girl arrived home, she devoured the food right from the pots and pans. And she talked and talked all about her day, her friends, her challenges and achievements. Mother listened to every word with smiling eyes and a proud heart.

Time ran as a river, but they did not feel it, as every day was lovelier than the day before. Girl grew and grew each day as Mother became smaller and smaller.

One day Girl decided she was big enough to go explore the world on her own. She shared her thoughts with Mother. Mother smiled. "Perhaps Girl was joking," she thought. "How can she go away when she is only a child?"

Ready for an adventure, Girl packed her bag. Mother cried and pleaded with her to stay, but Girl had made up her mind, and she was older now. She had her own dreams and desires. She wanted more than the little house could offer. Girl left with the birds and butterflies, with the wind and raindrops, with the river and the rising sun. She left.

The house became an empty nest for Mother, void as if nothing had ever been there. Every morning Mother arose early as usual. She cooked and cleaned, washed Girl's clothes, dried them, then washed them again. Mother waited for Girl to return any minute, hoped she was just joking, hiding somewhere as she did when they used to play hide and seek. The food grew old, spoiled, and was thrown away. And starting again the next day . . . same and same . . .

Days passed, then months, then years. Mother waited and waited. She grew tired and old. Finally, her patience bowl overflowed, and she decided to search for her child. Mother put on stone shoes, chose a thick tree branch for a cane, locked the door, and left. She walked through days and nights, becoming tired and thirsty. Just as the sun was rising, she arrived at a meadow. She asked the green meadow, "Oh, beautiful, open meadow, have you seen my child with eyes darker than the night, a smile sweeter than honey, and a voice softer than a feather?" The meadow did not answer.

When a breeze brushed the tall grass and passed on, Mother

kept going.

Before the sun was tall, she arrived at running river. She asked as a beggar, "Oh, tumultuous river, have you seen my child with eyes darker than the night, a smile sweeter than honey, and a voice softer than a feather?" The river did not answer, only growled away with all its might.

Mother washed her hands and face with icy cold water and rested a bit. "Traveler has to get going," she then said to herself and continued walking.

In the distance, Mother saw a mountain, its snowy top fading into the clouds. "Oh, mighty mountain," she said, "have you seen my child, with eyes darker than the night, a smile sweeter than honey, and a voice softer than a feather?"

The ancient, gray-headed mountain shrugged heavily, shattering into rocks, dropping down and hiding himself in the dust he made.

Mother had no choice but to keep walking. The night settled down and she sheltered under an old mulberry tree. The moon slowly rose, and bright stars emerged from night's womb. Mother raised her tired head to the sky and spoke slowly, for she was exhausted from the long days of hunger and thirst and constant worry. "Oh, you beautiful night sky, you ancient moon, and dearly shining stars, you are up high, you can see all around. Please tell me, have you seen my child with eyes darker than the night, a smile sweeter than honey, and a voice softer than a feather?"

The moon slowly closed her eyes, for she was ashamed that she had no answer for Mother, and the stars nervously giggled, shooting away.

After months of searching and asking, walking through high and low, rough and slow, the stone shoes were worn out and the cane was but a stub. Mother knew it was time to go back to her empty little home.

The house was colder and quieter than ever. Mother made a fire, boiled water for tea, and baked some bread, but nothing felt right. As the days passed, Mother's eyes began failing. Her legs slowed, her figure became stooped, and she lost her passion for life, her hope that her child would return. The house settled crookedly and dust gathered in every corner, but Mother didn't care, for she didn't want a house without her child. Mother became grouchy, complaining ceaselessly about everything, about how the food was tasteless, the house was cold, the days were long, and she was old. She complained and complained. Then she simply gave up, just sat there and waited for death to come and take her.

One morning the old, broken door creaked slowly open. When Mother turned her nearly blinded eyes to greet her death, there stood a beautiful young woman with eyes darker than night and a smile sweeter than honey. The woman spoke with voice softer than a feather.

"Hello, Mother," the woman said. Seeing the condition of her mother and the house, her heart sank and she rushed for a hug.

At first, Mother did not recognize the beautiful woman, but as she came closer, Mother's heart trembled. This was her child; she had returned, finally.

Mother opened her arms wide, but suddenly she recalled Girl's betrayal, leaving her mother for so long. Mother remembered searching for her, all those long days and nights, lonely and tiresome years. She became angry and pushed her away.

Mother spoke bitterly, "I don't need you anymore, I'm fine without you. I waited so long for you." She grumbled, complained, cried, judged, blamed . . . then she quieted.

The young woman said nothing; she waited for Mother to pour out the troubles of her heart. When silence filled the room, she slowly rose from the floor and hugged her mother. After a brief silence, Mother raised her eyes and looked at her; this was the same child with eyes darker than the night, a smile sweeter than honey, and a voice softer than a feather. Now Mother hugged her back.

It was as if time had not passed, as if nothing had happened. Mother and Girl both felt it; they both knew. First there was love, and love was always there.

I'll sing a lullaby to bring you sleep
May a rose's petals take you in
And inside those rose's petals
May you find a sweet dream
Lullaby, my little flower, lullaby
My sweet child, lullaby

THE MOON CHILD

Sadagat Aliyeva

ONCE THE WORLD WAS TALL and she was small. There were millions and millions of people all around her.

Millions of feet were busy walking, walking to millions of places, but there weren't enough feet to walk with her. Millions of hands were busy doing, doing millions of different things, but there weren't enough hands to stroke her hair. Millions of eyes were busy watching, watching millions of interesting things, but there weren't enough eyes to look at her. Millions of tongues were busy chatting, chatting about millions of important things, but there weren't enough tongues to tell her something nice.

She was alone. Sometimes she liked to be alone, but most of the time she wished she had somebody.

While the millions of bodies lay sleeping at night, she sat on her bed and gazed at the Moon. And the Moon looked back. She thought to herself that the Moon too was alone.

One night, while staring at the Moon, she heard a smooth and silky voice. The Moon was calling her. The Moon's voice was like running water, like a lullaby she had never heard before. Then the Moon's rays began falling down to her. They looked like arms, thick and strong, beckoning her to climb them, to climb them up to the Moon—the Moon who knew her name.

"Come to me," the Moon said to her. The voice was so kind and soothing, but she had a fear in her little heart. Nothing like this had happened to her before. Nobody even lifted her or held her anymore. She looked at the Moon, and the peaceful, motherly smile gave her comfort and courage. She stepped on the bright, soft moon rays and began carefully climbing. She climbed and climbed. And the Moon smiled at her. The Moon's smile was big and warm; it smelled like baking bread.

"Don't be afraid," the Moon whispered. "I will hold you tight. I will not let you fall. Keep climbing."

And the stars, they were waving and giggling all around the

96

Moon. Their music sang out, "Hello-o-o-o-o-o, cute one. You've got star eyes like us, and you can fly like us."

"Yes, yes, do as the stars say," the Moon added. "Fly instead of climb."

She tried. And she flew. She flew and flew. The rays were bright and kind, lifting her ever higher . . .

She visited the Moon every night. The Moon held her, and they walked all around the sky, jumping on the soft, fluffy clouds. The Moon told her funny stories about her star children and silly clouds with her silky voice, and she laughed and laughed. Sometimes the moon rays tickled her feet, making her giggle like the stars. She heard her own voice, little, soft, and jingly, and wondered if she had ever heard her own voice before. Down there. When she became tired and sleepy, the soft moon rays flew her back, enveloped her bed, and rocked her to sleep.

One night, when she was visiting the Moon again, there were more dark clouds around her than before, and the stars reminded her of the jellyfish she saw under the water when she swam in the sea. She loved the sea; swimming and jumping over the huge waves always excited her. Now the soft motion of the dark clouds resembled the rolling of the deep, dark sea. She wanted to swim and catch the jellyfish.

"Go ahead," the Moon whispered in her ear.

"What?" She looked at the Moon with amazement. "How do you know what I am thinking?"

"I just do," smiled the Moon. "Now, go on."

She looked at the deep, dark sea again. "What if I fall?" she thought to herself. Her little heart filled with fear.

The Moon read her mind again. "You won't. You should never be scared." The Moon smiled. "I'm always with you." Soft rays purred against her dark, curled hair. "Trust me, always," the Moon whispered gently.

The Moon's words warmed up her little heart. Her eyes watered from the kindness and her little arms wrapped the Moon. With one last little hesitation she looked at the sea, and she jumped. She jumped from one cloud to another chasing the jellyfish, the laughing

stars. While swimming through the sky, she felt the Moon's long, soft arms around herself, saving her from falling, protecting her from harm.

Millions of years passed by. During these years the Moon kept her company while she grew. One day, she heard a different voice calling her. It couldn't be the Moon; it wasn't time for the Moon.

She heard her own voice again when she answered the call, a bit different, somewhat dull, for she was older now. She saw a young man standing in front of her, nervous and shy, asking her hand. Also nervous, she reached out her hand. The man held it gently and they walked together through a crowd, hearing a voice saying, "I pronounce you man and wife." She understood she would not be alone again. Two teardrops rolled down her cheeks. She looked at the Moon that night, and she was sure there were teardrops in the Moon's eyes too. But the Moon smiled at her as always.

As years passed, she had millions and millions of children. She became busier with walking, talking, patting, looking, feeding, holding, and kissing. Before bed, she told stories to her children about the Moon, about swimming through the sky among the stars. Listening the stories, the children grew with starry, moonlit dreams.

Days weren't always the same. Some days she was overwhelmed and exhausted, lonely and fearful. Sometimes children got sick or hurt, making her sad. At those times, when she felt helpless, she always closed her eyes and listened, and she heard the Moon's soft and comforting voice in her heart: "I'm always with you. Trust me." The Moon's calming voice and soothing words lifted her heart, brightened her eyes, and brought ease to her day.

As they all grew together, it felt as if she were the Moon and her children were the stars around her; they would jump and dive, climb and fly, giggling together . . .

Millions of years passed. The children grew taller and moved in different directions. As she got older, she couldn't move fast or do all the things she had done before. She was alone and rested most of the time.

One summer night, she stepped outside as she heard a familiar, dear voice calling. The beautiful full Moon spread her arms all around, kissing the treetops. Millions of stars were shining brighter than ever. Her face lit up as she saw that big, warm, milky smile. The Moon was calling her to fly again, but she couldn't move anymore. The Moon reached out her long arms, wrapped them around her, and lifted her from the ground. And she started flying slowly.

She flew in the moonlight. She knew this was her last flight. Her eyes welled up, for she was happy. And the Moon was happy too.

They hugged each other.

She was a Moonchild after all.

AY UŞAĞI

Sadagat Aliyeva

BIR ZAMAN DÜNYA UCA, o balacaydı. Ətrafında çoxlu-çoxlu adamlar vardı.

Milyonlarla ayaqlar elədən beləyə, belədən eləyə gedərdi, amma bir cüt ayaq tapılmazdı ki onunla gəzməyə çıxsın. Milyonlarla əllər gecə-gündüz cürbəcür işlərə məşğul idi, amma bir cüt əl tapılmazdı ki onun saçına sığal çəksin. Milyonlarla gözlər milyon cür maraqlı şeylərə baxardı, amma bir cüt göz tapılmazdı ki onu da görsün. Milyonlarla ağızlar dayanmadan mühüm şeylərdən danışardı, amma bir dil tapılmazdı ki onu şirin bir sözlə dindirsin.

Beləliklə o tənhaydı. Bəzən bundan xoşlansa da çox zaman istərdi ki onun da kimsəsi olsun.

Gecələr hamı yuxuda ikən, o yerində oturub Aya baxardı. Bəzən öz-özünə fikirləşərdi ki Ay da onun kimi tənhadır.

Belə gecələrin birində, Ayı seyr edərkən, yumşaq və zərif bir səs eşitdi. Ay onu çağırırdı. Ayın səsi axar su kimiydi, ana laylası kimi. . . O hələ heç zaman belə bir səs eşitməmişdi. Sonra Ay qızılı şüalarını aşağı endirməyə başladı. Ana qolları kimi möhkəm və nəvazişli görünən şüalar onu dırmaşmağa, birbaşa Ayın yanına qalxmağa təhrik edirdi. O Ayın ki onun adını bilirdi.

"Gəl yanıma," Ay nəvazişlə səsləndi. Bir anlığa onun canını qorxu bürüdü. Həyatında hələ heç zaman belə bir şey baş verməmişdi, Çoxdandı kimsə onu qucağına belə almamışdı. Amma Ayın simasında ovundurucu və eyni zamanda cəsarətləndirici bir şey vardı ki onu irəli addımlamağa sövq etdirdi. Balaca ayağını çəkinə-çəkinə parlaq və zərif ay şüaları üzərinə qoydu və ehtiyatla dırmaşmağa başladı.

Yuxarı, yuxarı, yuxarı. . . Qalxdıqca qalxdı. . . Ay da ona baxıb gülümsəyirdi. Ayın böyük ve iliq təbəssümü ana südü kimi, təndirdə bişirilən çörək təki qoxuyurdu. "Qorxma," Ay pıçıldadı, "mən səni tutmuşam. Heç vaxt sənə yıxılmağa imkan vermərəm. Qalxmağa davam et."

Hələ ulduzlar . . . Ayın ətrafında pıqqıldaşıb ona əl eləyən ulduzlar. "Eyyyyy, balacaaaa. . ." ulduzların səsi musiqi kimi göyə yayılırdı. "Sənin gözlərin ulduz kimidir," ulduzlar yene pıqqıldadılar "bizim kimi. Həm də bizim kimi sən də uça bilirsən əlavə etdilər." "Hə, hə, ulduzlar düz deyir,"Ay əlavə elədi, "uç, sən uça bilərsən."

O cəhd elədi, və özü də təəccübləndi. Uçmağa başlamışdı.

Uçduqca uçdu... Uluzlaırın ətrafında dövrə vurdu. Hara gedirdisə, Ayın şüalrını ətrafında duyurdu və şüalar ona daha da yüksəklərə qalxmağa yardım edirdilər...

O gündən hər gecə Aya qonaq oldu. Ay onu əlləri üstündə bütün səma boyu gəzdirirdi, yumşaq buludların üstündə tullanır, ulduzlarla qaçdı tutdu oynayırdı. Ay ona öz ipək səsi ilə məzəli nağıllar danışır, o da güldükcə gülürdü. Bəzən Ay şüaları onun ayaqlarını qıdıqlayardı. O da ulduzlar kimi pıqqıldayar və bu zaman öz səsini eşidərdi, yumşaq, balaca, cingiltili səsini. Təəccüblənərdi ki, əvvəllər heç zaman öz səsini eşitməyib, orada, aşağıda. . . Yorulanda nəvazişli Ay şüaları onu geriyə, öz otağına gətirər, yüngülcə yırğalayıb yatırardı.

Bir gecə, yenə Aya qonaq idi. Bu dəfə ətraf qara buludlarla tutulmuşdu. Həm də ulduzlar ona yay aylarında üzdüyü dənizin dibindəki meduzaları xatiırladırdı. Dənizi cox sevərdi, üzməkdən, boyük dalğaların üzərindən atılmaqdan çox xoşlanardı. İndi bu tutqun buludların yumşaq gərdişi ona eynilə dərin və qaranlıq dənizin ağır-ağır tərpənişini xatırladırdı.

Ürəyindən üzmək, meduzaları qovub tutmaq keçdi. "Nəyi gözləyirsən, baş vur," Ay pıçıldadı. Üzünü çevirib təəccüblə Aya baxdı, "Mənim nə fikirləşdiyimi sən nədən bildin?" soruşdu. Ay nəvazişlə gülümsədi, "Eləcə bilirəm," dedi, "İndisə durma, dəniz səni gözləyir." O yenidən gözlərini çevirib ağır-ağır tərpənən tutqun dənizə nəzər saldı, "Bəs birdən yıxılsam," deyə fikrindən keçirdi. Balaca ürəyini qorxu aldı. "Yıxılmayacaqsan," yenidən onun fikrini oxuyan Ay pıçıldadı, "sən heç vaxt qorxma, Mən hər an sənin yanında olacağam." Ay gülümsəyərək əlavə elədi və yumşaq şüaları ilə onun tünd qəhvəyi, balaca hörüklərinə sığal çəkdi. "Sən mənə inan."

Ayın sözləri onun körpə qəlbinə hərarət gətirdi. Gözləri

yaşardı, balaca qollarıyla Aya sarıldı. Sonra son çəkingənliyini boğub dənizə atıldı. Meduzaları qova-qova bir buluddan o birisinə tullandı. Səma boyu üzdükcə, Ayın sevgisini, hərarətini, onu necə yıxılmaqdan, əzilməkdən qoruduğunu daima hiss etdi.

Milyon illər beləcə keçdi... Bu illər ərzində onun necə böyüyüb ərsəyə çatdığına Ay şahidlik elədi.

Bir gün yenə bir səs onu çağırdı. Amma bu Ayın səsi deyildi, tamamilə başqaydı. Çağırışa cavab verəndə öz səsinə təəccübləndi, səsi də özü kimi böyümüşdü. Həm də elə bil cingiltisini itirmişdi. Sonra bir gənc onun əlini tutdu. İzdiham boyu irəlilədikcə kiminsə "Mən sizi ər və arvad elan edirəm" dediyini eşitdi. Bir daha tənha olmayacağını anladığında gözləri doldu və iki damla göz yaşı yanaqları boyu diyirləndi. Həmin gecə Ayın da gözlərinin yaşardığına tamamilə əmin idi. Amma Ay həmişəki kimi yenə də gülümsəyirdi...

Günlər günləri, illər illəri əvəzlədi. Milyon milyon uşaqları oldu. Bu illər ərzində başı körpələrinin qayğısını çəkməyə, yedirməyə, gəzdirməyə, danışmağa, dinləməyə, qucaqlayıb öpməyə, layla çalmağa qarışdı. Hər gecə yatmazdan qabaq balalarına Ayla görüşlərindən, gecələr səma boyu üzməsindən, ulduzlarla qaçdı-tutdu oynamasından şirin şirin nağıllar söylədi. Onun bu nağıllarını dinləyə dinləyə balacalar ay işıqlı, ulduz pıçıltılı bir dünya ilə boyüdülər.

Günləri həmişə eyni olmazdı. Hərdən həddindən çox yorular, hətta tənhalıq, qorxu hissi keçirərdi. Bəzən də körpələrdən hansınınsa xəstələnməsi, yaxud yıxılıb əzilməsi onu çox məyus edərdi. Belə vaxtlarda, özünü kimsəsiz, köməksiz hiss edəndə, həmişə gözlərini yumar və Ayın yumşaq və təsəlliverici səsini eşidərdi, Mən həmişə burda, yanındayam. Mənə inan. Bu səs onun ürəyinə rahatlıq, gözlərinə işıq gətirərdi.

Bəzənsə ona elə gələrdi ki, o özü Ay, uşaqlarsa ulduzlardır. Birlikdə oynar, tullanıb düşər, dırmaşar və üzərdilər. Hey gülər gülərdilər... ulduzlar kimi.

İllər keçdikcə körpələr böyüdülər və bir-bir müxtəlif səmtlərə üz tutdular. O isə qocaldı. Yavaş yavaş gözləri işıqdan, dizləri taqətdən qaldı. Daha əvvəlki kimi nə sürətlə yeriyə bilir, nə də evvəllər gördüyü işləri etməyi bacarırdı. Günlərinin çoxunu dincəlmək, yatmaqla keçirərdi.

Bir yay gecəsi az qala unutduğu doğma səsə oyandı. Ehmalca yerindən qalxıb ayaqlarını sürüyə-sürüyə çölə çıxdı. Əsrarəngiz bütöv Ay öz qızılı süalarını yarpaqlardan süzüb aləmi xəfif işığa bürümüşdü. Milyonlarla ulduzlar Ayın ətrafında həmişəkindən daha artıq parlayırdılar. Ayın böyük, yumşaq, və südqoxulu təbəssümü onun simasını işıqlandırdı, qəlbini həyəcanla doldurdu. Ay yenidən onu çağırırdı, amma o nəinkə uça, hətta addım belə ata bilmirdi. Bunu görən Ay qollarını aşağı uzadıb ona sarıdı. Ayaqları yerdən üzüldü və Ayın köməyi ilə yenidən uçmağa başladı.

Ay işığında uçduqca uçdu və anladı ki daha bu uçuş əbədidir. Gözləri sevincdən yaşardı. Ay da sevinirdi. Bir birinə sarıldılar.

Hər şeyə rəğmən o elə həmişəki Ay uşağı idi. . .

MELISSA PALMA

ARTIST STATEMENT

I grew up in the rolling cornfields of the Hawkeye State in Waterloo, Iowa. The people in my community and the city I come from are rooted in histories of displacement.

The ancestral lands of the Meskwaki people who suffered the violence of settler colonialism are where my grandparents would visit the casino in Tama. The descendents of the German, Irish, and Norwegian immigrants in the mid-1800s became my parochial elementary school classmates. The African-American communities that can trace their families' Great Migration out of the Jim Crow South in the 1920s and the Bosnian refugees who fled civil war in the 1990s were my public high school peers.

As an Iowa-raised daughter of Filipino immigrants, the places where I find community are varied and diverse. Despite our extensive history with the United States, Filipino-Americans often grapple with issues of erasure and colonial mentality. Inundated by messages equating assimilation with success, I witnessed how the effects of race, class, and language can twist one's fate. It is revealing to call a place home that no one expects you to be from.

While most Filipino American history and literature focuses on communities in California and the West Coast, this project serves to document stories of migration and the many paths we take to call Iowa home. I am honored to participate in the inaugural Bicultural Iowa Writers' Fellowship. I hope to share a piece of my own family's story among the rich tapestry of transnational identities in Iowa.

My professional training has taught me to become a witness to human narrative and its deep potential for healing. I dream of broadening the definition of who is an Iowan and what we value, definitively proving that we are not other people's children, but rather, we are the future of the state.

MI ÚLTIMO ADIÓS

Melissa Palma

Speak, *anak*—
Of unsung heroines
Whose compassion imbued Pampanga's fertile riverbanks

Fleeing the Japanese War and the Marcos Regime
To Hacienda Florencia, whose stewards will forevermore
Profess symbols of love and devotion

Speak, *Hesukristo*,
And share the legacy of inheritance

The seasons passed, and the time came
For Libertad to offer the *novena* prayers
With dear *mga pamangkin* surrounding her
As she, her daughter, and her granddaughter were sent forth

Traversing oceans and prairies,
Becoming diaspora,
Until she too relinquished her own native land

There her daughter tended to the Americans,
In the heartland of the country without name
Now an Overseas Filipino Worker, curator of remittances,
No longer *doktora*, there she remained, losing her accent

And the granddaughter
Matriculated in the halls of the patina campus,

Where the Defining American was speaking
Of countless souls, in legacy
Colonialism had silenced
To their implied inquiry
"We are here because you were there"

Speak, *Ate*
She voices but a lick of the mother tongue
Yet prattles on like a *conquistador*

When she came of age and coveted her heritage, the
Parting words of Rizal resounded,
"¡Adiós, Patria adorada, región del sol querida,
Perla del mar de oriente, nuestro perdido Edén!"

But the Castilian farewell meant nothing to *ang pamilya*

Bahala na
Hindi ko po alam

ORD TO CID

Melissa Palma

I FIRST SAW THE SON on my way through the TSA security gate. A small hand scrubbed off the fuchsia imprint of his mother's lips from his cheek, his complexion that of the undulating Chocolate Hills from his ancestral lands. Ang galing naman! A Filipino boy of perhaps age five or six. His face stared back at me, haunted as the Visayan blood, I assumed, that flowed through his veins. Holding a papaya-orange tablet, complete with foam bumper case to guard against the enthusiasm of childhood, he was adorned with a penguin-shaped cross-body satchel and a winning smile.

He waited for his sister as they approached the podium; a security agent careened down at them from her brushed-metal watchtower. My gaze fell on maliit na batang babae; she appeared to be the same age as her brother and carried a bumblebee-shaped tote half her size. Her long, black hair was carefully plaited atop the crown of her head and cascaded down her back. Wearing an onyx Michael Kors puffer jacket and quilted Ugg boots, she was paying full attention to her own mango-colored tablet, which she cradled like a doll.

To my surprise, their sandy-haired mother followed, sporting dragon-fruit-pink highlights and floral-embroidered over-the-knee riding boots. She had the look of a person who, in her college days, majored in Gender, Women, and Sexuality studies. Now, fulfilling her destiny as a woke womxn of the Resistance, she spent her mornings frying cage-free eggs sunny-side up for her children while casually retweeting bell hooks and Roxane Gay.

Her husband ushered them forward in line to the security checkpoint. Were it not for the Bluetooth Jawbone headset tucked behind his ear and the Chiclet packet snuggled in his breast pocket, he would be a walking L.L. Bean advertisement. Decked in a sturdy persimmon flannel and a trim beard, he had a distinctive look that said, "I know how to light a campfire in the rain."

I was unable to fully compute the backstory of this multihued family, which left me restless, scavenging for clues. As a flight attendant distributed golden junior pilot wings to the little ones, I scanned for telltale signs of infertility. The mother was of solid build and wore matte concealer—perhaps polycystic ovarian syndrome? The father's ample facial hair dissuaded any notion of hypogonadism on his part. The parents seemed young, albeit with seemingly abundant resources for adoption. Was she of advanced maternal age?

I had so many impertinent questions. How much IVF did they shell out for before turning to an overseas orphanage? Or did they choose adoption, purporting ethical notions of conserving environmental resources? Were they the kind of parents who bought a house in the West Liberty school district to enroll their kids in bilingual schools? Kung kausapin ko ba sila sa kanilang sariling wika, sasagutin kaya nila ako sa Ingles o Tagalog? Or would I merely face blank stares of confusion?

This halo-halo family, my Precambrian brain ever wanted to categorize them into boxes and silos for which I had little precedent. Unlike my friends from more rural parts of Iowa where international adoptees were the norm, I grew up cocooned by the idea that Asian children belonged to Asian families. Even in other blended households, if one parent were an American GI Joe while another parent a nurse, their hapa children were always rooted by food, by family, by Filipinos.

I noticed them again upon boarding the aircraft. Leaning forward with as much discretion as I could, I watched as parents and progeny sat two by two in separate rows. Nakakagigil talaga ang bata, the adorable ones seated in front, each engrossed in their individual black mirrors of distraction on their laps. I stifled a giggle as their entertainment devices loudly blasted cartoon theme songs. Scowling, the returning snowbird in the aisle seat next to them couldn't properly enjoy her gulp of airplane whiskey (two Templeton Rye, neat).

The parents held hands in the row directly behind. I judged them instinctively. Walang hiya, why doesn't she sit up front with her children? *Like a real mother,* I added parenthetically, and was immediately ashamed.

Midway through the predeparture safety video, I heard a

gleeful squeal and saw a plastic trinket catapult into the air. The wing-shaped pin landed in the lap of a hirsute man with prominent sideburns who was knitting on circular needles. He uncrossed his legs and returned the airline token to its guardians. In response, the mother drew her face close to the son and whispered sympathetic words of warning punctuated by a kiss atop his shiny bowl cut.

I pondered their future and how they would grow up. Would they, too, be the Only Ones in their suburban Midwestern world? Would they eschew arroz caldo and sinigang in favor of Pop Tarts and Chef Boyardee to avoid lunchroom ridicule? Would they internalize their Wonder Bread surroundings and become *those* adoptees? The ones who wake up and tell the world from their brown faces that, "Sometimes I forget I'm not white until I look in the mirror in the morning."

Would they inherit their parents' presumed neocolonial tourism practices, embodying the privilege of unencumbered and unquestioned travel as a consequence not of their contributions but the mere color of their passports?

Backpacking through Southeast Asia with fresh eyes and an old soul on a gap year, would they simultaneously experience both discovery and homecoming while dodging volcanic ash on their way to conquer Mount Bulusan? Documenting their adventures with a GoPro trekking along the Banaue rice terraces, would they bother to notice the eroding numbers of Ifugao farmers who remain grounded in the land?

My questions were never ending. But as I pulled back from the wide-angle lens in my mind racing at light speed, I slowly reeled in the many piña threads I had woven into the fabric of an imagined future for these young ones I had never met.

I stole one last look. The children were laughing as their parents gingerly passed apple slices through the gap between seats 7B and 7C. In that moment I saw nothing more than a loving family, and it was beautiful.

ORD SA CID

Melissa Palma
Translated by Marissa Bender

UNA KONG NAKITA ANG batang lalaki noong ako ay papunta sa pasukan ng seguridad ng TSA. Pinupunasan ng isang munting kamay ang mapulang marka ng labi ng kanyang ina sa kanyang pisngi, ang kanyang kulay katulad ng umiindayog na mga Chocolate Hills sa kanyang bayang pinagmulan. Ang galing naman! Maaring siya ay isang batang Pilipinong may lima o anim na taong-gulang. Ang kanyang mukha'y nakatingin sa akin na taglay ang dugong Bisaya, na palagay ko'y nananalaytay sa kanyang mga ugat. May hawak na tablet na kulay papayang kahel, na may-kutsong matigas na takip upang pangalagaan laban sa kalikutan ng bata, siya ay pinalamutian ng isang mala-pinguinong maletin na nakabalot sa katawan at ng isang nakabibighaning ngiti.

Hinintay niya ang kanyang kapatid na babae habang papalapit sila sa mesa, isang ahenteng pangseguridad pababa sa kanila mula sa kanyang tila-kinaskas na torreng bakal. Ako ay napatingin sa maliit na batang babae, siya ay waring kasing-edad ng kanyang kapatid na lalaki at may bitbit na hubog-bubuyog na bayong na mas malayong malaki kaysa sa kanya. Ang kanyang mahabang itim na buhok ay maingat na nakatirintas sa tuktok ng kanyang ulo at lumagaslas sa kanyang likod. May suot na kulay onyx na chaketang makapal na Michael Kors at mala-kutson na botas na Ugg, siya ay taimtim na nakapokus sa kanyang kulay-manggang pansariling tablet na kanyang kinargang parang isang manika.

Sa aking pagkamangha, nakita ko ang kanilang inang may mala-buhanging buhok na sumusunod na may kulay-rosas na highlights sa buhok at burdadong bulaklak na botas pangkabayo na lampas-tuhod. Wari siyang isang tao na, noong kapanahuhan ng kanyang pagkokolehiyo, ay nag-aral tungkol sa Kasarian, Kababaihan, at mga tema ng Sekswalidad. Ngayon, habang binubuo ang kanyang kapalaran bilang isang makapangyarihang babae ng Laban, ang kanyang mga umaga ay ginugugol sa pagprito ng mga itlog ng malayang manok na plastado ang pula para sa kanyang mga anak habang walang pagkabahalang nagrere-tweet ng mga bell hooks at Roxane Gay.

Inakay sila ng kanyang asawa pasulong sa linya upang lapitan ang checkpoint ng seguridad. Kung hindi sa Bluetooth Jawbone na headset na nakatago sa kanyang tainga at ang pakete ng Chiclet na nakasukbit sa kanyang bulsa sa dibdib, siya ay matatawag na naglalakad-na-patalastas ng L.L Bean. Ang ama, na nakasuot ng matibay na kulay persimmon na pulang pranela at maayos na balbas, ay may sadyang hitsura na malinaw na nagsasabing, "Alam ko kung paano magsindi ng apoy sa kampingan sa ulan."

Hindi ko maunawaan ng buo sa aking kaisipan ang kasaysayan ng makulay na pamilyang ito, na nag-iwan sa aking di-mapalagay sa paghahanap ng mga sagot. Habang nagpapamahagi ang flight attendant ng mga ginintuang laruang pakpak ng piloto sa mga batang musmos, naghanap ako ng mga palatandaan ng pagkabaog. Ang ina ay mukhang malusog at ang mukha ay nabahiran ng pampatago ng taghiyawat, maaari kayang may sakit na polycystic ovarian syndrome? Ang makapal na buhok ng ama sa mukha ay nag-alis sa pagpapalagay na baka may hypogonadism sa kanyang bahagi. Ang mga magulang ay waring bata, subalit parang may maraming mga pagkukunang yaman para sa pag-ampon. Tunay kaya siyang nasa edad na maaaring maging ina?

Napakarami kong impertinenteng mga tanong. Gaano kaya karaming IVF ang kanilang nagasta bago nila napagpasiyahang mag-ampon ng bata sa ibayong dagat? O pinili ba nila ang pag-ampon dahil sa diwang etikal ng pagsanggalang sa mga pangkapaligirang yaman? Sila ba ang uri ng mga magulang na bumili ng bahay sa distrito ng paaralan ng West Liberty para ipatala ang kanilang mga anak sa paaralang bilingguwe? Kung kausapin ko ba sila sa kanilang sariling wika, sasagutin kaya nila ako sa Ingles o Tagalog? O sasagutin lamang ba ako ng mga nalilitong blangkong titig?

Ang pamilyang halo-halo na ito, nais isauri ng aking utak-Precambrian sa mga kahon at kubo na kung alin ay halos wala akong paghahambingan. Hindi katulad ng aking mga kaibigang galing sa mga bahaging mas probinsya ng Iowa kung saan ang pandaigdigang mga batang ampon ay karaniwan, ako ay lumaking nailihis sa kaisipang ang mga batang Asyano ay ukol sa mga pamilyang Asyano. Kahit sa mga magkahalong tahanan, kung ang lalaking magulang ay isang Amerikanong GI Joe habang ang babaeng magulang ay isang nars, ang kanilang mga anak na hapa ay laging nakaangkla sa pagkain, sa pamilya, sa mga Pilipino.

Napansin ko uli sila pagpasok sa eroplano. Bumaling paharap hangga't kaya, na di nagpapatawag-pansin, masusi kong pinagmasdan habang ang mga magulang at anak ay umupong pandalawahan sa magkahiwalay na hanay, ang nakakapanggigil na mga bata'y nakaupo sa harapan, bawat isa nakatutok sa kanya-kanyang sariling kandong na mala-salaming itim na gamit-panlibangan. Pinigil ko ang pagbungisngis habang ang kanilang mga gamit-panlibangan ay malakas na nagpatugtog ng mga temang kanta ng cartoons. Kunot-noo, ang bumabalik-sa-upuan na matandang-snowbird na nakaupo sa upuang pang-pasilyo na katabi nila ay hindi maganahan ng husto sa kanyang pag-inom ng whiskey ng eroplano (dalawang Templeton Rye, walang halo).

Magkahawak-kamay ang mga magulang sa direktong likod na hanay. Sa isip ko, agad ko silang hinusgahan. Pambihira naman, bakit hindi umupo ang ina sa harap kasama ng kanyang mga anak? Dagdag kong panaklong at kaagad napahiya sa sarili ko, "Tulad ng isang tunay na ina."

Sa kalagitnaan ng bidyong pangkaligtasan bago-lumipad, nakarinig ako ng isang masayang ingit at nakita ko ang arko ng isang plastik na bagay na lumipad sa himpapawid. Ang hubog-pakpak na de-aspileng laruan ay lumapag sa kandungan ng isang balbas-saradong mama na may makapal na patilyang nagniniting gamit ang bilugang mga karayom. Inayos niya ang kanyang de-kuwatrong upo at isinauli ang naturang laruan sa mga may-ari nito. Bilang sagot, inilapit ng ina ang kanyang mukha sa batang lalaki at malambing na bumulong ng salita ng babalang may kasamang halik sa itaas ng kanyang makintab na mala-mangkok na gupit.

Nagmuni-muni ako tungkol sa kanilang kinabukasan at kung paano sila magsisilaki. Sila rin kaya ay magiging Nag-iisang mga Batang palalakihin sa kanilang lugar sa suburbia ng bahaging Midwest? Tatalikuran kaya nila ang arroz caldo at sinigang kapalit ng mga Pop Tart at Chef Boyardee upang maiwasang laitin sa kantina ng paaralan? Kukulubin kaya nila ang kanilang paligid na Wonder Bread at maging isa doon sa mga uring iyon na batang ampon? Yaong mga batang gigising at ipagsisigawan sa buong daigdig ng kanilang mga kulay-kapeng mukha na, "Minsan ay nakakalimutan kong ako'y hindi puti hanggang sa tumingin ako sa salamin sa umaga."

Mamanahin kaya nila sa kanilang mga magulang ang kanilang ipinalagay na mga kaugaliang panturismong neo-colonial, nangangatawan sa pribilehiyo ng walang-sagabal at walang kuskos-balungos na paglalakbay bilang bunga hindi ng kanilang mga kontribusyon kundi sa pamamagitan lamang ng simpleng kulay ng kanilang mga pasaporte?

Habang naglalakbay na naka-backpack sa Timog-Silangang Asia taglay ang preskong pagtingin at lumang diwa sa isang taon ng puwang, sabay kaya nilang mararanasan kapwa ang pagdidiskubre at pagbabalikbayan sabay-iwas sa abo ng bulkan papanhik sa Bundok Bulusan? Pagkakaabalahan kaya nilang pansinin ang bilang ng kumokonting mga magsasakang Ifugao na nananatiling nakaangkla sa lupa habang itinatala ang kanilang mga pakikipagsapalaran gamit ang isang GoPro samantalang tinatahak ang lawak ng Hagdan-hagdang Palayan ng Banaue?

Walang katapusan ang aking mga katanungan. Subalit sa aking pag-atras sa malawak na anggulong-lente ng aking isip na matuling tumatakbo, dahan-dahan kong hinatak-pabalik ang maraming sinulid ng pinya na aking tinirintas sa isang tela ng pinangarap na kinabukasan para sa mga batang musmos na ito na ni hindi ko man lamang nakilala.

Panakaw akong tumingin ng panghuling beses. Ang mga bata ay tumatawa habang ang kanilang mga magulang ay magiliw na nagpapasa ng mga piraso ng mansanas sa pagitan ng puwang ng mga upuang 7B at 7C. Sa sandaling ito wala akong ibang nakita kundi ang isang pamilyang mapagmahal, at ito ay tunay na napakaganda.

FILIAL BONDS

Melissa Palma

KHRISTINE RIVERA WALKED WITH PURPOSE across the Pentacrest in the central campus of the University of Iowa through a golden whirlwind falling from gingko trees. A senior majoring in international studies and political science, she was, as usual, incredibly busy. The former Fil-Am teen beauty queen and all-state speech and debate champion perused the agenda of her upcoming week. Brushing the fan-shaped leaves from her jacket, she scrolled through her meticulously color-coded academic, family, and social calendars.

In time with the rising sun, a notification chimed. Reading the notice, she gave a sigh and an eye roll of exasperation. In a rare lapse of judgment, she had allowed her roommate to set up a Heart2Heart profile. Pushed by the latest online dating app, the banner cheerfully exclaimed, "Are you ready to meet your match?", accompanied by a picture of the day's most eligible 20- to 26-year-old, cisgendered, heterosexual males within a 0- to 25-mile radius of campus.

As an Asian woman dating online, she knew the odds were in her favor. Centuries of Orientalism under the Western gaze had done its damage depicting her sisterhood as subservient flowers. She expected to halfheartedly acquiesce to a slurry of dates of varying quality with an overabundance of otaku white boys who watched too much *Naruto*.

Based on the lackluster profile descriptions, without even looking through the pictures, she declined most of their invitations to chat. The 22-year-old enabler of science and discovery at an agribusiness conglomerate, resident Instagrammer, and youth translator to his middle-aged colleagues? Swipe left, denied. The 25-year-old MD/MBA candidate who lived and breathed medicine, at least until he cashed out to the most promising Silicon Prairie health-tech startup? Swipe left, denied. The 20-year-old K-pop B-boy wannabe boasting of three nights in the Polk County jail for street performing without a permit? SMH, swipe left!

118

Khristine always told herself that nothing serious, of course, would detract from her ten-year plan. Intern as a White House Fellow. Gain admittance to a top law school. Become the first Asian American woman from Iowa to serve in the U.S. Senate. Amplify the voices of struggling people from immigrant families like hers. Make a difference in the world. She was a woman with purpose who could not waste a moment on trifling romance.

And then, she met Dean.

∽

Dean Chung was a level-headed ombudsman and agnostic Unitarian Universalist minister-in-training. As a graduate student, his research focused on the sociology of nonreligious second-generation Chinese Americans. They almost never met, save for his invitation to go out for hand-pulled noodles and explore the wonders of the university library's special collections room. In truth, it was the original Edna Griffin papers in the Iowa Women's Archives she was longing to meet.

A native of the East Bay, he followed his mother to the University of Iowa, where she was an otolaryngology department chair who valued long-term therapeutic relationships with her patients. Khristine and Dean shared stories about their immigrant families, his Han Chinese and hers Tagalog and Maguindanao Filipino, and the lives of hardship they would never know in the lands their families left behind. Together over a shared bowl of lāmiàn, they lamented not only their inadequate command of their mother tongues but also the fact that asking their parents to teach them would be met with admonition rather than instruction.

Their first date continued to the library special collections, where they pored over aged newspaper clippings describing the 50th anniversary of the successful effort to desegregate Katz Drug Store in 1949 by Edna Griffin, the Rosa Parks of Iowa. As they discussed Edna's courage, Dean confessed that he always wanted to be in Gryffindor, the Hogwarts House famed for bravery, but was actually a Ravenclaw. Khristine told him that she always wanted to be in Ravenclaw but was actually a Hufflepuff.

119

Among the stacks, she learned that he majored in philosophy at Stanford and savored the art of conflict mediation. He wanted to know why she felt so uncomfortable being thought of as an authority figure despite her many accomplishments and ambitions. She gave him her often-told reply, "Because of my stature and gender, I am never granted positions of authority without fighting for it."

Feeling at home among books, she explained how, for the first time, she saw a piece of herself in fiction while reading Celeste Ng novels. Unlike his California upbringing, she identified with being the Only One in a small Midwestern town. Growing up in the Bay Area, he had never experienced microaggressions for speaking unaccented English until he came to the Hawkeye State.

With a knowing look, Dean asked if she was a writer. Khristine thought to herself, "Is it how I talk? Or maybe how I gush over books?" She would be sad the day she would have to call herself a citizen emerita of the City of Literature.

∽

Not long afterward, when midterms were over (hers taking, his grading), they met downtown for dinner. Dean explained how the nonreligious composed over one-fifth of second-generation Chinese Americans, including himself, and his quest to help people like him lead meaningful, ethical lives. Using his generational cohort as a framework to understand cultural duty and deep respect by way of the Confucian tradition, they could find higher meaning through the narrative of the family.

Passing rainbow rolls between chopsticks, dropping only every eighth, Khristine and Dean sketched diagrams of their bookshelves and their personal organizational schema: "You situate Poverty and Inequality Studies next to the Asian American History section?" "I much prefer placing Yang's graphic novels next to Morrison and Bulosan on the Marginalized Identities shelf." On the backs of napkins stained by wasabi, they drew maps of California, the Midwest, the Mainland, and the Archipelago connected by a web of arrows to illustrate where their stories came from.

120

Khristine had never felt so connected to another person so effortlessly; she longed to imbibe further details about his life. After hearing of his aversion to Maid-Rite sandwiches, she learned that he was a pescatarian. He was a photographer for his high school newspaper. He spent a summer after college as a camp counselor for children with autism. In undergrad, they called their tony Palo Alto campus "The Farm," and it was the most rural place he had ever lived until Iowa.

He asked how she interpreted her identity as a Filipino-American who was culturally Catholic. She told him about her first expressions of gender identity wearing plaid jumpers at the behest of her mother in kindergarten, then wearing only pants in a small act of rebellion until middle school. While she texted a classmate to coordinate a group project, a glance at the Totoro home screen on her cell phone made him smile. He took her out for dessert, both ordering taro boba tea, and eagerly made plans to meet again.

∽

They next came together at the IMU Black Box Theater, to be present and receive the presence of ReOriented Words, the longest-running Asian American open mic tour in the Midwest. She had never heard anything like it before. From the banal to the sublime, it was such a gift to see herself and their collective stories reflected onstage in slam poetry.

The comedic monologue of the Mindy Kaling-wannabe was a bit too saccharine for her palate, but she snapped enthusiastically all the same. Whisky Saigon Girl was a true poet, throwing shade on those who equated Vietnamese cuisine with phở alone. Her identity reduced to a piece of food, she was the resistance to be consumed. Finally, they were wowed by the featured Gao Vang, a sage of the stage who memorialized the tragedy of her little sister via sonnet. She with the courage to call out, "American Family Values? Bullshit. America is a country where children move across the country for college."

These diasporic performers plucked their heartstrings so deeply, vibrating at the wavelength of the universe. So many sighs and affirmations. So much love and humanity in that sweltering room, emanating into the depths of the night.

As the masses exited the theater onto the street, the crown of their heads touched but for a moment as Khristine and Dean gazed at the stars. They had both seen the Milky Way, but not the Northern Lights. He promised someday they would. As he walked her home, ever so slightly out of step, she noticed him staring longingly at church towers and naves, yearning for community, filling each breath with the weight of forgotten ghosts of the Cultural Revolution.

༺

As she finished editing her latest policy report on the economic feasibility of needle exchanges for harm reduction in the opioid crisis, Khristine was unusually excited to meet Dean for the monthly First Friday reception. At the Museum of Art, they marveled at the multitude of musical instruments from various eras, attempting to divine their function from form. Passing by what could have been his great-great-grandfather's erhu or her grandmother's kulintang, they learned that they both competed as defense attorneys at state mock trial tournaments.

Dean smuggled in gỏi cuốn, and they snacked on spring rolls that tasted altogether too healthy. He shared that he was named from a baby book in English, though his name was chosen to be easy for Mandarin speakers to pronounce. She told the tale of how she her name was a portmanteau of her maternal grandparents' names, Cristosomo and Tinay.

He argued at her dismissal of participatory budgeting anywhere but at the municipal level. Evoking the boondock mountains from the clues of "remote, rural, military," he divined his first Tagalog word, bundok. She lamented how the phrase seemed to be the only relic from the Philippine–American War to remain in common parlance, or even remembered at all.

They meandered through exhibits of found-plastic palaces that shimmered as the gilded present from a broken past. Dean thought about 义务 as they sat in a velveteen room. He paused, and then blurted, "I'm moving back to California, full disclosure."

"When?"

"Soon."

Her heart fell.

She said that she was fine.

She was not fine.

Attempting to regain control of a swell of unnamed emotions, Khristine, as planned, reached into her bag. She wanted to lend him her favorite possession, a neurosurgeon's memoir on living a virtuous and meaningful life in the face of premature death. Dean was reluctant to accept the dog-eared book. He said that he didn't want to do any false advertising.

Ignoring his statement marking their limited time, in response she asked him to interview his grandmother, like he had always wanted. Turning toward a celadon basin on a pedestal, she pretended to read the fine print of the label to hide the emerging redness on her face. She stoically told him to record his nǎinai's wisdom, as she had done with her own lola on her most recent trip to Quezon City.

"You have to," she said. "Family is so important."

⌇

Reflecting on their time together, Khristine was refreshed by Dean's lack of imposter syndrome due to self-professed luck, privilege, and hard work. This philosophy was in deep contrast to her own insecurities and incessant need to compare herself to the bevy of exceptional people in her surroundings.

She was studying for the LSAT over Thanksgiving break when he sent her a draft from his manuscript.

I realize a great proportion of our spiritual hurt stems from a misunderstanding of our ethical inheritance. As long as we believe our "Asian values" are a rigid set of codes, we fall into the false trap of choosing between our parents' values and the values of the society we live in as Americans. But if we reflect and understand the framework that our contemporary inheritance stems from, we realize the East Asian humanist tradition is, in fact, one of the most dynamic and insightful sources of wisdom for living meaningfully in the modern era.

Although he found the perfect blend of what he wanted to do in this world in ministry and mediation, at times the roar of the Tiger Mother echoed throughout his inner monologue. During those moments, he felt the draw to enter the medical space because there was so much good to be done.

On the day classes resumed after Thanksgiving break, Dean told her how he was almost lost to the industrial medical complex. He spent the year before grad school helping his cousins run Crista Galli Care, a preventive medicine startup hoping to topple the colossus. His mother, the surgeon, called preservation of the patient's story the most important tool in the vast armamentarium for diagnosing and treating disease. They spoke of art and family and duty. He let her know that he was moving back to California in a few short weeks.

"When?" she asked, although she did not want to know the answer.

"Graduating at semester." He hesitated. "They need me now more than ever."

༄

Khristine smiled with her face but not with her eyes on the day in December she asked him to a concert at The Mill. Knowing that their paths were now diverging, they entered the bar together to hear Kishi Bashi perform ethereal ballads on looped violins.

Politely pushing through the stream of humanity advancing toward the stage, she enjoyed the rush of sound washing over them. The throng of bodies of the crowd made it difficult for either of them to see, but, oh, could they hear the anguish of this indie multi-instrumentalist. Dean placed a hand on the small of her back to keep balanced. She leaned into him to take in the details of the prismatic light and synesthesia and being so close to the origins of melody.

Walking side by side along the just-salted sidewalk, his phone rang jarringly as he hurried a few steps ahead. She watched from afar as his brow knit together in concern, and as she approached, she heard a ghostly sob. It was the call he had been dreading; his father's mother was sick in the hospital in Richmond. Throughout the night, his family sent a flurry of texts, his phone a chorus of sorrow as she comforted him with a warm pot of chicken adobo.

∽

Khristine and Dean met for the last time near the boathouse on the winter solstice, although she did not know they had finally reached their apogee. They walked uphill toward campus through twinkle-light trees along manicured paths shortly after a snowfall. She asked him if her loaned book about the terminally ill neurosurgeon was too much, but it was the childhood arrivals in deferred-action limbo for whom he shed tears.

Although meant for children, they climbed playgrounds of modular hexagons and compared their mismatched sizes. Continuing their journey along Riverside Drive, they stood feet to feet on the bridge overlooking the Iowa River and gazed at the moon. Together, they saw the arc of the universe bending toward justice.

They sipped their warm drinks, slurped gummy tapioca pearls, and spoke about the difference between artisanal, artistry, and craft. He smiled as he showed her a photo of his hometown's páifāng gateway, adorned with four serendipitous characters, draped by American and Chinese flags. She nodded in silent agreement. The perfect book cover.

And thus, the chapter of Dean Chung, humanist extraordinaire, ended. Khristine Rivera thought to herself about the whirlwind of these past few months, "My, how the boy has left a mark on my soul." He said goodbye with a parting hug and returned her book for good. Afterward, he said that he was glad to have met someone so humanistic in politics. Khristine turned the corner to leave and gulped down the remainder of her boba tea. It tasted bitter and cold.

CVA

Melissa Palma

1 | THE FATHER'S STROKE

Dr. Danilo Socorro Magno woke up on a Thursday morning. The room was silent around him, save for the quiet echo of a distant radio from the kitchen downstairs. He wiped the rheum from his eyes and rolled over to greet his wife. His hand lay empty in the soft impression where she had risen from bed hours before. "I forgot," he thought to himself. "She must be teaching her tai chi class at the senior center today."

The physician's hand fumbled for his eyeglasses on the bedside table. He placed the wire frames on his wide nose bridge, and the world came into focus. He smiled at the platter of coffee and soft-toasted bread laid out before him. As was their ritual, his wife had prepared breakfast at the bedside for when he awoke.

"Salamat, ha. I'm thankful she knows I like my toast with both butter and sugar, even though I'm sure my primary would prefer she didn't," he said to himself. Chuckling at the idea of a doctor who needs a doctor, he added, "At least I don't take creamer in my *kape!"*

Dr. Magno consumed his black coffee and pandesal while listening to the morning news on public radio. He rose from bed, massaged the cricks from his right knee, and made his way to the shower before dressing in a crisp shirt and an unassuming pair of slacks. Kneeling to rub the calluses on his heels from decades of long-distance running, he quietly traded his house tsinelas for proper loafers at the door. Always planning his next actions, the physician envisioned himself taking the road leading away from their sleepy subdivision as he had done without fail for the past twenty-six years in the country.

The jolt of caffeine was invigorating as he started the car. His amplified sensory acumen detected the trace scent of freshly laid fertilizer that wafted over from the farm down the road. He ran through a brief mental list of patients he planned to see that morning.

"My 34-year-old female with granulomatosis with polyangiitis and a penchant for jazz music. My 55-year-old female with stage V CKD on dialysis who painstakingly knit wool hats for each of my nurses last Christmas. My 89-year-old male with uncontrolled hypertension who races turtles with his grandson at the Rotary Club."

As a practicing nephrologist taking care of chronically ill patients, Dr. Magno had come to know many details of his patients' personal lives. Always with the utmost professional candor, of course. Both he, and the community, would expect nothing less.

On his way to clinic, he drove past alternating postage-stamp plots of corn and soybeans on either side of West 4th Street. He revved the engine for a bit of fun as he was nearing the familiar turn and the driveway of United Medical Park.

But then, in a second, he wasn't.

Overcome by dizziness, he found himself in the parking lot of the Hy-Vee several blocks away without knowing how he got there. His mouth curled around an unrecognizable sound thrust out by his tongue.

His clinician's mind quickly built a differential. Sudden-onset unilateral vision loss accompanied by vertigo and slurred speech. Transient ischemic attack, central retinal artery occlusion, generalized seizure, cerebral vascular accident. An ominous voice that he could not recognize as his own portended, *"Ay naku po.* I think I'm having a stroke."

2 | THE DAUGHTER LEARNS

The physician's daughter was sitting in the third-floor atrium of the medical education library. She liked to study in the sunlight, looking out across the Iowa River and daydreaming about being anywhere but here. The table was strewn with reams of course notes, each page meticulously highlighted, color coded, and categorized.

Jojo Magno was waist deep in renal physiology, rapidly calculating acid-base practice problems and trying to remember whether

Winter's formula was to be applied before or after the correction for bicarb. A fourth-year medical student at the University of Iowa, she was studying for the medical boards, a twenty-six-day marathon that would be the culmination of everything she and her parents had hoped to achieve by moving to the States.

The musical crescendo of Debussy's "Arabesque No. 1" rang in the background; instinctively, she rummaged through the backpack to answer her phone. Her fingers fumbled over the cool steel of her stethoscope, the gummy triangular head of her reflex hammer, before finally reaching the smooth glass of her cell phone. A missed-call notification from her mother flashed on the screen.

She swiped through her voicemail transcription and sighed. It never could decipher her mother's accent. "Transcription Beta (low confidence). Hi _____ Joy. You might be _____ driving _____ careful love _____. Bye."

Crepuscular rays from the setting sun cast shadows on Jojo's computer screen. Her mind was full and she took a much-needed break to call back hours after the initial message. The phone rang once on the other end of the line. Her mother's hurried voice explained in a flurry of English and Tagalog. The daughter was dumbfounded. "What do you mean, he's been in the hospital for three days already? Why didn't anyone tell me?"

Maria Milagros Hilario Roque Magno was once a lawyer herself in the Philippines before relinquishing her profession to become a mother in a foreign land. She attempted to calm her increasingly histrionic eldest child. "*Anak*, we didn't want to worry you. We know you are studying very hard and we didn't want to distract you."

In an instant the young medical student, who had spent years accumulating objective scientific knowledge of the human body, knew absolutely nothing. Only that her father was seriously ill and she was powerless to change it.

3 | THE DAUGHTER RETURNS

The future Dr. Josefina Nyota Roque Magno sped ten miles over the speed limit along the entire length of I-380 north on her somber sojourn home to Waterloo, Iowa. The gleaming silver grain silos and majestic timber-frame barns on the roadside became an imperceptible blur. She received updates from her mother via speakerphone and immediately regretted the first thought that came into her mind: "Oh my god, he needs to be transferred to the university."

In a reversal of roles, she had become one of her patients' concerned family members. An instant archetype, the ones who looked to the storied University Hospitals and Clinics as a cathedral of healing. To them, it was a place where miracles happened, where people were given a second life.

Intimately familiar with the personal sacrifices required to achieve such miraculous recoveries, her reasoning was much less noble. Even to Jojo, ever the optimist, the hospital was a place where souls, of both patients and providers, went to die.

Instead, she simply told her mother, "I'm afraid he won't get impartial care at home."

It was true. The distinguished Dr. Magno knew all of the physicians in their midsized Midwestern city where he had built his practice and raised his family for the past two decades. Many of them, like him, were international medical graduates who migrated to rural parts of America where doctors are scarce and need is always growing.

Their office parties were a veritable United Nations of the heartland. The Cuban family doctor married to a Filipina oncologist met on a medical mission trip. The Sikh nephrologist who oftentimes covered her father's call schedule, but only if her own kids weren't sick. The Bosnian neurologist who, when she was seven years old, would bring chocolate milk to the call room as Jojo and her four-year-old brother invented puppet shows with no-slip hospital socks while their father was busy seeing consults late into the night.

Although the daughter had not visited any other countries besides her parents' native Philippines, she traveled extensively via her taste buds throughout childhood without ever leaving the Cedar Valley. Whenever a new physician's family moved to town and came over for dinner, their home would be filled with a joyous blend of her family's suka and patis along with the inviting aromas of their guests' garam masala or berbere or za'atar spices. Jojo wondered which one of their former houseguests was presiding over her father at this very moment.

Her mother's disembodied voice interrupted the memories. "Everything will be fine, *anak. Bahala na.* Just pray to God, He will provide."

4 | THE FATHER PRONOUNCED

Jojo arrived at the ICU to the sound of her mother wailing.

She had flashbacks to her last rotation as a medical student in the MICU of the tertiary care center. Her first patient was dead before the team had even started rounds. She was an 89-year-old female with past medical history of rheumatic heart disease admitted for dyspnea on exertion, hypoxic respiratory failure, and a not-so-surprising acute on chronic loss of moxie.

In the dawn of the morning while scrolling through masses of data at her computer workstation, she had dutifully gathered vital signs of one already devitalized. Sketching out blank templates in the shape of fishbones and crosses, she copied down the patient's electrolyte and hematologic laboratory values. All that was missing to complete her pre-rounding was a perfunctory interview to listen to the heart and lungs.

But unbeknownst to Jojo, her patient had already passed sometime in the night. Startled by the absence of the familiar S1-lub and S2-dub, she strained her ears and pressed firmly with the diaphragm. Still a learner, she adjusted the rubber ear tips of her stethoscope. The student took a sharp breath of her own and hoped to become attuned to the unmistakable clarity of lungs by auscultation, but she instead found fixed and static silence.

Dead? Her first patient on her first day of her first ICU rotation in medical school? Instead of helping the resident document the progress of her patient's notable recovery, she learned how to write a death pronouncement. She feared that once-buried knowledge would now resurrect itself.

"Ano ang nangyari?" asked her mother's shaking voice as she

watched her firstborn stand frozen in the doorway. The daughter stepped over the sterile threshold and noticed her little brother, still in his work uniform, asleep on the couch.

Jojo gazed downward in shame at her mother's inquiry. She didn't have an answer. She didn't have any answers.

In the ICU of the medical floor where she once played make-believe, her father lay still in a hospital bed. His eyes were closed, but she could still discern a slight asymmetry of his facial muscles, a laxity of limbs on his left side. Instead of the man who had taught her how to expertly mix a sidecar and change a car tire, in his place she saw a ghost in a shell.

Periwinkle gown askew, his body was unceremoniously uncovered like a child who had outgrown his favorite clothes. The man who boasted about running a ten-minute mile on his fifty-fourth birthday was now propped up by pillows on either side of his torso. Like so many other patients she examined in the wee hours of the morning, he would have looked completely anonymous were it not for her own mother sobbing at his bedside.

Still coping with the gravity of the situation, she did what she was conditioned to do in times of crisis. She dissociated herself from the sentiment and immersed herself in the technical to become her family's advocate. Although they were trained professionals, it had been over a quarter century since anyone else in her family had staffed the inpatient units. They needed someone, they needed her, to interpret his maladies. Moving methodically, Jojo began assessing her father's deficits.

Once conscious, Danilo became more alert and keenly responsive. He could blink his eyes and follow the tip of her finger with a smooth gaze both horizontally and vertically. Peripheral confrontation testing revealed that his field of vision was much reduced. Although he could squeeze her hands upon command, she noted a much looser grip on the left. The patient was able to achieve grade four motor strength in the right arm and leg but could only muster grade two range of motion with gravity eliminated on the left side. When asked to name the month and state his age, she could barely make out a garbled phrase.

Startled by his loss of language, Milagros brought her daughter closer and asked her husband, *"Sino ang siya?* Danilo, who is this?"

His mouth pursed to point in her direction as he struggled to speak.

"Oo. Oo."

Milagros nodded and leaned in, removing herself from her husband's newest blind spot. "Yes, yes? Can you understand me? Who is she?"

Danilo scrunched up his face with great effort and attempted again, "Yo-yo, yo-yo."

Her mother's eyes lit up. *"Mahal,* I think he's trying to say Jojo."

While clinically predictable given the diagnosis, the father's physical exam was devastating to the daughter. Dysarthria, homonymous hemianopsia, facial hemiplegia, unilateral hemiparesis. These were all words she had seen hundreds of times in lecture notes and textbooks, but they did not become real until applied to her beloved Tatay as he faced an end of the life they had once lived.

When Dr. Sharma came in the next morning to convey information from her latest consultations with the neurologist and the cardiologist, Jojo had given up all pretense of objectivity. The only thought running through her head was, "He can't even pronounce my name anymore."

5 | THE REHABILITATION

In aftermath of the cerebral vascular accident, details emerged that Jojo wished she did not know. On the third day, she was told that her father arrived to urgent care and was quickly identified by the triage nurse as having an acute stroke. Hurriedly ambulanced to the local emergency room for evaluation and a CT scan, he was given antiplatelet medications and clot-busting injections within two hours of symptom onset upon consultation with Dr. Sarkic.

As a professional courtesy, he was directly admitted to the inpatient medical floor, but to the dismay of his care team he was never issued a hospital ID band identifying him as a patient until well after his admission.

Tying her box braids out of her face, the nurse questioned, "How am I supposed to take care of my patient when I can't even open a package of gauze without any identification?" Exasperated, she continued, "No ID band, no MRN, no nothing. What do y'all think this is, a hospital or a hotel?"

From her introduction to health systems course, the daughter knew this was how medical mistakes happened. First the deviation from protocol, then inadvertently missing important allergies, then a near miss, and then a catastrophe. Like perfectly aligned holes in Swiss cheese, the culmination of errors would haunt her father as he was whisked away to the MRI suite.

On the eighth day of his recovery, Jojo sat for the medical boards. That morning, her hands wouldn't stop shaking to the point where she would have failed a test for dysmetria. Over the course of nine hours she miraculously managed to complete all of the questions on the exam without bursting into tears. She would do her fair share of crying when the scores were released in four months' time. But at that moment, when the emotions got hold of her, all she could think about was how her life of privilege was so closely teetering on the edge.

Before the event, she thought her margin of error was as wide as the continents her family migrated across, fleeing oppressive regimes. The guilt of her complacency was drowning. "My parents were my age when they started over." She wiped away the salinated liquid pooling in her eyes and chastised herself for being so selfish. "I knew one day I would have to take on familial obligations. I just didn't think it would be so soon."

Thirteen days after, she crossed herself and began her neurology rotation on the stroke service. She was privileged to witness a seasoned attending gather the family of a recently transferred patient. Kneeling to eye level with those seated before him, he looked directly into their eyes with intention before calmly counseling all present, including her.

"There are three stages of treatment after a stroke. The first stage is here in the hospital where she will be monitored until stable by my excellent care team. The second stage is at the rehabilitation center to learn anew her activities of daily living. And the third, and most important treatment of all, is when the patient returns home to grapple with a host of marital, social, and spiritual issues that lie within the stewardship of you all, her beloved caregivers."

On day 34 in rehab, Danilo was brought to daily speech therapy. His diet was advancing, albeit slowly, from liquid to soft mechanical. He was in physical therapy (ter in die), and his wife was closely taking notes during each session as they recorded his gait velocity. Milagros was determined to augment her enfeebled husband's physiotherapy and learned techniques to encourage predictable, repetitive movements and exercises. They would shape his brain circuits with the right experiences to rewire them, akin to infant development. It was not the first time she had taught someone how to walk.

The patient returned home on day 89. In preparation, his son removed all area rugs to protect against bone-breaking falls. A family friend installed a wheelchair ramp in the garage and handrails in all of the bathrooms. Unanimously, the remaining members of the household decided to retrofit the elder daughter's old bedroom on the ground floor with the hydraulic patient lift and hospital bed.

Instead of celebrating a joyous reunion with her family on the day of his homecoming, Jojo was sitting in an empty hotel room in Minnesota on the interview trail for residency positions. She called her brother to video chat to remind him to save her a plate of pancit. It was the first time she saw the sterile railings of the patient's new bed juxtaposed against the ballet-pink flounces framing her childhood window.

Without a greeting, she commanded, "Let me talk to *Tatay*, Paolo." Flipping his Panthers baseball cap from backward to forward, the younger sibling snipped back, "Okay, okay. *Ate*, don't have a *carabao*," as he positioned the screen in front of his father's body.

By all accounts, he was in a recovery of sorts. Conversations with her father had become easier to understand but more painful for her to endure over the past few months as his speech difficulties ossified.

Danilo used to cherish the turn of phrase or a play on words in any language. He would devise games to quiz his children on

134

the Latin roots of medical terminology. When concocting bedtime stories, the purported monster would be banished by the heroine's bilingual declaration, "You shall terrorize children no more across this land, by the powers that be, *ang nakakatakot* is now *nakakata-cute!*"

As time passed and his English began to fail him, it was her strange language that was taken only literally. With her mother and her brother at her side at the medical college on day 233, Jojo called to tell her father she had matched to the family medicine residency in Waterloo. She was coming home!

One month prior, compiling her rank list was an agonizing task. Although she had once dreamed of attending a prestigious residency at Mayo Clinic or Mass General to study geriatrics, their new life and her reduced stock required a recalibration of priorities. Her dreams were different now. She would be there for them, and for him, until the end. Duty, honor, service. Always.

Disappointingly, but as expected, their family's inside jokes and her good news fell on a stranger's ears over the phone. She feared he now had difficulty understanding humor, that he was immune to joy. The daughter wondered how much longer they had until he no longer recognized her face. Until he no longer recognized any of their faces. Until he no longer recognized himself.

6 | THE EMISSARY

The young medical student, Danilo Socorro Magno, thumbed through the pages of his DeGowin Bedside Diagnostic Examination guide to the physical examination by flashlight during the latest brownout in Quezon City, Philippines. He was studying for the FLEX test, the first step in applying for medical residencies in the States.

He knew the odds were poor for a scholarship kid from the baryo who never quite fit in with the upper-crust families at school, but that never stopped him from achieving top marks. Even when his batch mates would snicker behind his back at the second-hand polos he bought from the ukay-ukay, it only drove him to work harder.

135

There were no tourists in Project 6. The tiny barangay, squeezed between Mindanao Avenue and Visayas Avenue, was constructed in the same utilitarian brutalist concrete as the rest of Metro Manila just north of EDSA. Next to the abandoned lot with the barking street dogs, the apartment block was dotted by sari sari stores of enterprising Filipinos hawking cola in plastic bags impaled by a straw.

The next morning as he hopped off the jeepney riding to campus, it happened again. Snatching the Coke-bottle glasses off his face and knocking over the tower of books he was carrying, his bully taunted, "Danilo was hit in the head with a dictionary!" He kneeled to gather his discarded spectacles and his copies of *Robbins Basic Pathology, The Silmarillion,* and *The Foundation* series. He found solace in the writings of Tolkien and Asimov. In both fantasy and science fiction, you could count on the brainy misfits to contribute more than just comic relief. Despite their so-called physical deficiencies, they were heroes. Heroes celebrated in song and lore.

Shoving his backpack into his locker at the University of the Philippines, Danilo raced from one end of campus to the other while devouring a quick snack. He nearly tripped over the rut in the sidewalk kinked by the root of the banyan tree. Milagros was waiting for him at the bottom of the steps to the library by the Oblation statue and heard his rapid footfalls approaching. Mimicking the posture of the bronze figure facing upward with arms outstretched, she warned him with her eyes closed. "Uy, Speedy Gonzalez, sandali lang. You might hurt yourself."

Milagros and Danilo were meeting for their usual run along Roxas Avenue from UP Diliman. Both professional students taking up law and medicine, respectively, they were constant companions since becoming partners for their organic chemistry laboratory as undergraduates. Danilo was in awe of her superb percent yields; she gained top marks reconstituting colorless, odorless liquids into iridescent dreams. Milagros was drawn to his kindness, a quiet constancy in the chaos of their mega metropolis.

The young woman brushed off the lengua de gato crumbs from her running partner's Fernando Valenzuela jersey, which he wore religiously to their weekly ritual. She asked playfully, "Hoy pare!

136

Do you ever wash this thing?" He looked down at his Dodger-blue garment with the number thirty-four emblazoned on his chest. A gift from his cousin, an OFW living in California, it was a souvenir from a trip that represented his most cherished memory. Or at least, it would be until the end of today.

Jogging through the oppressive smog and congestion of the city center, the pair settled into an easy rhythm. She was the only one of their batch mates who matched his cadence, though he towered at least a good 14 centimeters over her. Growing up in the mountain highlands of Cagayan gave her the advantage, he assured himself.

Their usual route was shaded by the occasional palm tree and interrupted by the more frequent traffic jam. His heart quickened even though their pace slowed rounding the park in QC Circle.

Danilo reviewed the plan over and over in his mind. He had arranged for a taho vendor to meet them at the halfway point. He would suggest they stop for refreshments at the lake near the wildlife center and take in the sights. While she paused to enjoy the sweet, silken tofu drink, he would bend down on one knee to propose a lifetime of partnership. After pooling their savings for a few years and praying to avoid the growing power of Marcos's martial law, they would go to America together once he passed the boards and she passed the bar.

Lost in thought, he didn't even realize Milagros had picked up speed and was now 50 meters ahead entering the Hardin ng Mga Bulaklak. Surrounded by orchids and sampaguita blossoms in the sanctuary, she turned back to look at him as if to say, "I dare you to catch up, pogi." The future physician filled his lungs with the smell of jasmine and ran after her. In her eyes he saw their future, and their future was limitless.

THE WOMAN IN THE AMBER MOON

Melissa Palma

Memory: four years old. Mommy is listening to the original London cast recording of *Miss Saigon* on double-disc CD. The heat is on in Saigon and on her stovetop. She holds my new baby sister on her hip and stirs a pot of Mississippi catfish adobo. I hide underneath the dinner table and watch her cook, and the make-believe village I come from seems so far away. I copy her and plunge a large wooden spoon into my leftover bowl of cheesy grits. I throw a glop onto the tile floor and cover it with a napkin and wait. I want to see what it looks like when it dries, but Pappy comes home from work and I run away to watch TV on his lap until I fall asleep. I repeat my game every time we have grits in the house. Mommy always asks why the floors in that kitchen are so sticky.

Memory: five years old. We move into our new house in Iowa. Pappy hasn't had a job in six months. He has one now. Mommy is so happy. He carries the three of us into the home. Mommy is in his arms and my sister and me hold on at his ankles. He stomps his way through the front door like a paper tiger and we all giggle and fall down. We run around the empty house calling dibs on each room until Mommy and Pappy show us our shared bedroom. Pappy is looking through his luggage to put on a Kenny G CD, but Mommy gets to the boombox first. They slow dance to a song played on a solo saxophone. My sister and me cover our eyes and hold our noses because they are being mushy. Yuck!

Memory: twenty-six years old. A trailer for the new Broadway revival of Miss Saigon was just released online. I search for it on my phone while shopping for a tam in my favorite vintage shop on the ped mall. I have mixed feelings about the show's latest run.

For my mother, and many Filipinos in the homeland and in the diaspora, the musical is a source of nostalgia and pride. It has launched countless careers of Filipino actors and actresses in musical

138

theater since its 1989 West End debut. For many refugees of the Vietnam War, each performance propagates harmful stereotypes. The entire production is a painful caricature of their country that contributes to the erasure of Vietnamese from their own narrative.

Memory: seven years old. It's the first day of first grade and I tell my teacher I want to be a Target cashier when I grow up. I like their red vests. It's recess and I get told that I have to play Pocahontas because I'm the only girl with black hair in our whole school. But I really want to be Meeko the raccoon because I like eating cookies and cherries and hair braiding too! But the boys made a deal and Johnny Thomas pushes me over because I don't want to do what he says and he tells on me to the recess monitor. I try to say it's not my fault, it was a trick! "You'd better prove it, and quick!" But now I'm in trouble and teacher gives me a warning and I have to spend the rest of recess in timeout on the blacktop.

Memory: eight years old. The movie in my mind plays a scene of Mommy cooking *Spamsilog* in the kitchen. She looks so pretty, just like Miss Lea Salonga on her CD case. She asks me how was my day, and I say that the kids at school asked if I will play Mulan this year for Halloween. And I told her that I must tell you no and that I really want to be Shelby Woo and solve mysteries and carry a giant magnifying glass. But no one has time to take me to the store and I'll just wear my school uniform instead.

She clicks her tongue in disapproval at the kids in my grade and tells me they are not nice, they're mostly noise, and continues humming more songs from her favorite soundtrack. I ask her what Miss Lea's musical is about. I do not yet know what the words *strip club, human trafficking,* or *Vietnam War* mean. She does not want to tell me either. She wants to inspire me to be more studious, to choose whatever heaven grants. Instead of the truth, she says, "They're in a school for girls, and it's dark because they don't have electricity. They have to sing to each other to communicate."

I laugh at the old-fashioned idea of studying by candlelight and chant, "Lights off, brownout! They are powerless!"

I listen to the pop-opera songs in the background and lick my lips and wait for the smells of Spam-infused garlic fried rice to rise with her voice.

Memory: twenty-six years old. Since college, I have educated myself about the show's problematic history. How Equity Actors in New York unsuccessfully protested the original Engineer's yellowface casting with signs reading, "Don't mess with my sister. Miss Saigon Serves White Man's Greed and Fantasy. We are real. Miss Saigon is not."

I learned from a friend's mother that the original lyrics to the marriage ceremony were complete gibberish, not even real Vietnamese words. They changed the translation in the newest version, but only at the behest of cast member Christopher Vo during early rehearsals.

Memory: ten years old. My parents are working and I am at day care. The big kids are allowed to sit quietly at the back table, so we finish our language arts homework and watch *Indiana Jones and the Temple of Doom*. Chris Scott points at the television and tells me he should be my new boyfriend. I scoff and want to say that I'm not a prize you can claim. I start to tell them Harrison Ford is older than my dad, but I look up at the screen and instead see the enthusiastic smile of Jonathan Ke Quan as Short Round screaming, "Hold onto your potatoes!" I blush and hide my face as the other kids laugh. This Vietnamese child actor of Chinese descent is the only Asian youth I will see on television for the next fifteen years.

Memory: fourteen years old. I'm in middle school and a touring company of *Miss Saigon* comes to Cedar Falls to perform at the Gallagher Bluedorn Performing Arts Center. By all accounts, the matinee performance is a Broadway spectacular. From the neon lights to the mesmerizing choreography to the holographic 3D helicopter landing onstage, the audience is amazed. During the fall of Saigon, as the Americans abandon the city, countrymen decked in salakot hats scream, "They'll kill who they find here! Don't leave us behind here!" My mom cries three times. I'm stunned for a

140

different reason. It's the first time I've ever seen anyone with my face in a starring role onstage.

Following the show, my parents treat my younger sister and me to dinner at Panera Bread. As we settle into our booth, my mom quickly recognizes familiar chatter in Tagalog, Cebuano, and Kapampangan. A large contingent of actors from the musical make their entrance, also seeking meriyenda for the evening.

My parents eagerly start chatting with the performers, and in in true Pinoy fashion, find out where their hometowns are located and if they know anyone in common. They swap stories of life on tour and how to survive an Iowa winter. My mom offers to bring baon for the homesick kababayan to snack on at their hotel just down the road.

Soon after, a new crop of theatergoers comes into the restaurant. They are also starstruck by the nearby table of raven-haired performers, still in full stage makeup and wearing matching *Miss Saigon*-branded warm-ups. They quickly approach to congratulate them on a spectacular show.

Then they approach where my family, clearly dressed in civvies, are devouring our You-Pick-Two meals with spoons and forks. They repeat their praise: "Oh, congratulations, you all really were just marvelous. This must be your American Dream!"

They walk away, oblivious, and my sister and I look at each other with exasperation. Even at this early age, we know this is the hour we must once again *prove* ourselves to our neighbors. Our parents laugh and, as dutiful daughters, we nervously join in. We don't know how to explain to them that this encounter is just like all the others. Another example of the invisibility of communities of color in the places we call home.

How in one night have we come so far?

Memory: twenty-six years old. Despite marketing of *Miss Saigon*'s many lyrical changes to suit "modern" sensitivities, you can't correct for the long-lasting legacies of French and American imperialism in Southeast Asia. You can't correct for the fact the Marine only calls Kim his girl but never his wife. You can't correct for one of the main characters, a Eurasian pimp, spewing self-hating lyrics claiming, "Greasy chinks make life so sleazy." Over time, I have come to realize that Asian participation in *Miss Saigon* is merely conditional.

Sometimes I wonder whether I would take my own future children to see my mother's favorite musical if it were resurrected yet again. Would they connect with its iconic logo, an Orientalized outline of a woman's face blended into a rising helicopter against the backdrop of an amber moon? To find versions of themselves onstage, I would hope they could instead support productions like Qui Nguyen's play, *Vietgone*; or George Takei's musical, *Allegiance*; or Sarah Porkalob's one-woman-show, *Dragon Lady*. Namely, theater written by people from, of, and for these communities themselves.

Maybe my children will grow up in a world where their stories will be more accessible. Or maybe they will even have the courage to one day write their own.

abuela/o/os—Grandma/grandpa/grandparents.

abuelita—A term of endearment for grandma, like granny or grandmama. Adding the suffix "ita" or "ito" creates a diminutive used to describe something small and/or cute, like the word for cat being gato and kitten being gatito.

alacrán—Scorpion. Card 40 in Don Clemente's Loteria card game. Also worthy to note el alacrán's significance in Mexican trinket culture, specifically its relationship to the state of Durango, directly south of Chihuahua.

araña—The Spider. Card 33 in Don Clemente's Loteria card game.

baile—A Mexican dance. Community bailes are a tenant of weekend social gatherings in Mexican culture.

cabrona—Strong insult. Cabron/cabrona is one of those fluid Mexican curse words that can run the gamut from term of endearment to stinging insult.

chamaca—Girl. Sometimes said with a bite; almost interchangeable with brat.

chambelán—Escort of honor to a quinceañera. The quinceañera party will pick out a group of male chambeláns and female damas as a court. Think awkward teenage bridal party. Many times the court will be painstakingly picked by the quinceañera; other times her elders will intervene and pick out participants as familial bargaining chips.

chicharrones de harina—Flour pork rinds, a popular snack of fried puffed wheat.

Chihuahua—One of Mexico's northern states bordering America. Many of West Liberty's immigrant families migrated from Chihuahua or its southern neighbor Durango.

coconut—Mexican American slang, derogatory for assimilated Mexican Americans (i.e., brown on the outside, white on the inside). Think of the term Uncle Tom for African Americans or twinkie for

Asian Americans.

code switching—Linguistic term describing switching back and forth between multiple languages during conversation.

el sol—The sun. Card 46 in Don Clemente's Loteria card game.

en el nombre de Jesús—"In Jesus's name." Said by many a strict older relative.

ESL class—English as a Second Language class. A precursor to the West Liberty School District's English Language Learners program (note the shift in focus).

guey—Pronounced like "way." One of the most used and fluid slang terms when referring to males. It can mean anything from dude to asshole to an exclamation of surprise.

Johnny Canales—A seminal radio DJ and television host of the music variety program The Johnny Canales Show in the 1980s and 1990s. Think American Bandstand for Tejano music. The horn section of the show's theme song is burned into the minds of many Mexican kids from the time period, as well as Johnny's English catchphrase of "You got it, take it away!"

Kimberly Park and Pool—One of West Liberty's main parks, complete with swimming pool. Growing up, we had bragging rights that ours was one of the only towns with both a swimming pool and movie theater.

Kirkwood—A community college in Iowa City. For many local Iowans, education at Kirkwood is the alternative to the University of Iowa, or a means to get the credits to transfer to the U of I.

Norteño bandas—Bands from Northern Mexico with roots in European musical styles, particularly German waltzes and polkas. This music can be regarded as the music of old school, traditional, rural Mexicans. It's the doot-doot music you hear when you pass by a Mexican BBQ. Some key bands are Los Tigres del Norte and Los Tucanes de Tijuana.

paletas—Popsicles.

paisa—Mexican slang, short for paisano, which translates as "countryman." Paisa is more of a soft derogatory word and fluid term of endearment. It translates somewhat to "hick." In Mexican American culture, it has become interchangeable with stereotypically unassimilated Mexicans.

Pelon Pelo Ricos—Tamarind-flavored Mexican candy. Loosely translates to "bald guy with tasty hair."

pinche—Strong cursing adjective used to enhance a statement (e.g., "pinche guey").

Rage Against the Machine—A '90s rock band, one of the first to mix rock and hip hop in a legitimate way. Known for their political stances and advocacy of marginalized groups.

Selena—Don't you dare think Gomez. The original Mexican American pop star, dubbed the "Queen of Tejano music" with hits in both English and Spanish.

Saludan a todos—"Greet everyone." A common maternal phrase. It's not so much that you have to say hello to everyone at a party or function, it's that you have to individually go and shake everyone's hand while doing so.

trocka—Texan/Northern Mexico slang for truck. If carro can be car why can't trocka be truck?

quinceañera—Formal celebration for a Mexican girl's fifteenth birthday, symbolizing her transition to adulthood. Quinceañera can refer to the celebration or to the girl herself. Its pomp and expense rivals that of a traditional wedding.

West Liberty—Iowa's first majority-Hispanic town, with a population of 3,736 at the 2010 census.

West Lib—Tongue-in-cheek slang for West Liberty, short for West Lib, Compton. Born out of the surrounding towns' irrational fear of West Liberty. Kids leaned into the town's persona, even though most of its residents will tell you West Lib is as safe as any other small town in America.

Zach de la Rocha—Rage Against the Machine frontman. The Mexican American son of Chicano artist Robert de la Rocha, Zach was one of the few contemporary rock musicians reflecting a Latin bicultural identity. Ritchie Valens for Generation X.

GLOSSARY | ALIYEVA

dolma—Azerbaijani food made with meat and greens wrapped in grape leaves.

dovga—Azerbaijani yogurt soup made with a vast variety of greens.

laylay—Lullaby.

pilov—Middle Eastern/Asian dish made with rice and different kinds of toppings.

stone shoes—Idiom used in Azerbaijani fairy tales to describe travelers' long walks from land to land.

GLOSSARY | PALMA

Filipino/Filipina/Filipinx—Person from the Philippines or of Filipino descent; over 100 million Filipinos live in the Philippines proper, while an estimated 10 million Filipinos live in the diaspora as migrants or Overseas Filipino Workers (OFWs) in countries such as the United States, Canada, Australia, Hong Kong, and Saudi Arabia.

Iowa—Named after Ioway, the French Word for the indigenous Bah-kho-je tribe, a landlocked state with boundaries that include the Mississippi River on the east and the Missouri River on the west; bordered by Wisconsin and Illinois to the east, Missouri to the south, Nebraska and South Dakota to the west, and Minnesota to the north.

Midwestern—Often perceived as General American English, this dialect may or may not be characterized by prevalence of the Northern Cities Vowel Shift; according to RAYGUN, LLC, of or relating to God's gift to planet earth and the galaxy's most important region.

Philippines—Named in honor of King Philip II of Spain, an archipelago nation of over 7,000 islands in Southeast Asia situated south of Japan, east of China, and north of Indonesia; the tropical country is divided into three main regions of Luzon, Visayas, and Mindanao.

Tagalog—National language of the Philippines, along with English; there are over 150 distinct languages spoken among the various ethnic groups in the Philippines.

THE FILIPINO FAMILY

anak—Tagalog, child, term of endearment.

ate/kuya—Tagalog, elder sister/elder brother.

kababayan— Tagalog, countryman.

lola/lolo—Tagalog, grandmother/grandfather.

mga pamangkin— Tagalog, cousins.

nanay/tatay—Tagalog, mom/dad.

pamilya—Tagalog, family.

tita/tito—Tagalog, aunt/uncle.

FILIPINO NATIONAL ICONS

adobo—National dish of the Philippines; a stew based on soy sauce and vinegar; from the Spanish adobar, "to marinate."

carabao—Water buffalo native to the Philippines; national animal of the Philippines.

Ferdinand Marcos (1917-1989)—President of the Philippines from 1965-1986; a corrupt dictator who declared martial law, engaged in extrajudicial killings, and swindled an estimated $5-$10 billion USD from the Philippine National Treasury; was ousted in the peaceful People Power Revolution demonstrations in 1986 and died in exile in Hawaii; however, his wife and children were allowed to return and have been elected to public office and political power.

José Rizal (1861-1896)—Filipino national hero, nationalist during the end of the Spanish colonial period, renowned polymath (political scientist, novelist, poet, sculptor, journalist, linguist, and ophthalmologist), and polyglot conversant in 22 languages (Spanish, French, Latin, Greek, German, Portuguese, Italian, English, Dutch, Japanese, Arabic, Swedish, Russian, Chinese, Greek, Hebrew, and Sanskrit, plus the local languages Malay, Chavacano, Visayan, Ilocano, and Subanun); author of the novels *Noli Mi Tangere* and *El Filibusterismo*, he was executed by a Spanish firing squad on December 30, 1896.

Lea Salonga (1971-present)—One of the most famous singers and actresses in the Philippines, first known for originating the lead role of Kim in the musical, *Miss Saigon*, in 1989; also served as the singing voice for iconic Disney princesses such as Jasmine and Mulan.

lengua de gato—Filipino butter cookie shaped like a cat's tongue, most famous in the mountain city of Baguio, a former site of Spanish, Japanese, and U.S. military bases.

sampaguita—*Jasminum sambac*; national flower of the Philippines.

IOWA STATE ICONS

Black Hawk County—Founded 1843, a county in northeastern

Iowa with a population of 131,090 in the 2010 census with the county seat residing in Waterloo. National Register of Historic Places in Black Hawk County include the Black Hawk Hotel, the Cotton Theater, and two Carnegie Foundation libraries.

Chief Black Hawk (1767-1838)—Born Ma-ka-tai-me-she-kia-kiak, a warrior of the Sauk American Indian tribe, and author of the first Native American autobiography in the U.S. in 1833; an active commander in the War of 1821 and the Black Hawk War in 1832.

eastern goldfinch—*Carduelis tristis*; the official state bird of Iowa.

Hawkeye—Common nickname for the state of Iowa, possibly originating from the eponymous scout, Hawkeye, in James Fenimore Cooper's The Last of the Mohicans published in 1826.

old rose—Along with black, the school colors of Waterloo West High.

puppy chow—Best-selling bake sale item in Iowa; a sweet concoction of cereal, chocolate, peanut butter, and powdered sugar erroneously named Muddy Buddies in the Chex cereal box recipes.

Wahawk—The official mascot of West High School, a portmanteau of the city and cFounty names of Waterloo and Black Hawk, respectively.

wild rose—*Rosa blanda*; the official state flower of Iowa.

LANGUAGE

barangay—Tagalog, neighborhood, the smallest administrative unit of government in the Philippines, also known as baryo, from the Spanish barrio.

bundok—Taglog, mountain; origin of the English phrase boondock, a rural town considered backward and unsophisticated, derived from conditions of guerilla warfare during the Philippine–American War of 1899-1902.

knee high by the Fourth of July—Midwestern English, what your eighth-grade science teacher says in addition to, "It's not a summer job, it's an adventure!" in futile attempts to get you to join his detasseling crew.

Kumusta po?—Tagalog, greeting, "How are you?"

not so bad—Midwestern English, said in response to "How are you?", conveys to the listener that things are positive, but the speaker does not want to appear boastful in their contentment lest it cause the listener to feel uncomfortable.

not so good—Midwestern English, said in response to "How are you?", conveys to the listener that the speaker is not at their best, but they do not want to burden the listener with the full details of why they really want to say "terrible."

piña—Tagalog, finely woven Filipino textile made from leaves of a pineapple plant.

ukay-ukay—Tagalog, secondhand store where items sold are commonly shipped from different countries including the United States. The author once saw a man in the Manilla on the MRT wearing an Iowa 2A basketball shirt prominently featuring the towns of Wapello, Sioux Center, Fort Dodge, and Ottumwa.

RAGBRAI—Acronym for the (Des Moines) Register's Annual Great Bicycle Ride Across Iowa, founded in 1973; roughly translates to 468 miles of sweat, determination, and the best rhubarb pie you'll ever eat next to 10,000 of your closest cycling friends.

Growing up in the Soviet Era of Stagnation and in a household ruled by anger, **SADAGAT ALIYEVA** always had a burning desire for freedom. She was drawn to the arts, poetry, and spirituality as a child and teenager to escape the reality around her that she couldn't bear. Her desire for freedom eventually brought her to the United States. Although Sadagat had a higher education in theater, she had to start all over again in middle age by learning a new language and new life. She graduated from the DMACC Graphic Design program in 2012. Sadagat lives in Des Moines with her husband, three teenage children, and two cats. She's a librarian at the Clive Public Library.

Sadagat describes America as a land where dreams can grow freely. A vast variety of experiences throughout her life inspire Sadagat to tell stories and draw. Her folktale-like stories draw attention to the beauty and wisdom in human nature.

MELISSA PALMA is an Iowa-raised daughter of Filipino immigrants. She was privileged to grow up in a multigenerational household with her grandparents, parents, and little sister in Waterloo, Iowa. Following graduation from the University of Iowa with degrees in biochemistry and medicine, her capstone project for the Humanities Distinction Track was the first to focus on the intersection of dance and patient communication. Her writing has been featured by *In-Training Magazine*, *In-House Magazine*, and now the inaugural Bicultural Iowa Writers' Fellowship. Melissa tweets @ IssaPalma.

JESUS "CHUY" RENTERIA is an artist, writer, dancer, and teacher, but above all, he is a storyteller. Born in Iowa City and raised in West Liberty, both sides of his family are from border towns in Mexico that transplanted to meatpacking towns in the Midwest. Growing up in West Liberty, he oscillated between the Mexican, Laotian, and small-town cultures that made up Iowa's first majority-Hispanic town. Chuy tells stories celebrating the spaces between cultures, of mangled Spanglish and generational clashes, of the messiness of people finding themselves. In addition to his writing, Chuy is an adjunct faculty member teaching hip-hop dance for the University of Iowa Dance Department and is the Public Engagement Coordinator for Hancher Auditorium.

ANDREA WILSON is the visionary founder of the Iowa Writers' House, an organization that has connected thousands of writers to new opportunities within the Iowa literary community. She developed the Bicultural Iowa Writers' Fellowship to provide an avenue for our newest citizens to share their stories and to allow audiences the chance to hear them. Her own writing approaches topics of belonging, culture, and tradition. In addition to serving as the executive director of the Iowa Writers' House and the editor of this collection, she has edited and published *This Is Our Peace*, an anthology on nuclear nonproliferation, and *Girls Making Magic*, an anthology of works by aspiring female writers aged ten to fourteen.